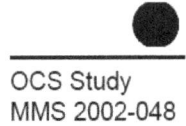

OCS Study
MMS 2002-048

Coastal Marine Institute

# Development of Bioremediation for Oil Spill Cleanup in Coastal Wetlands

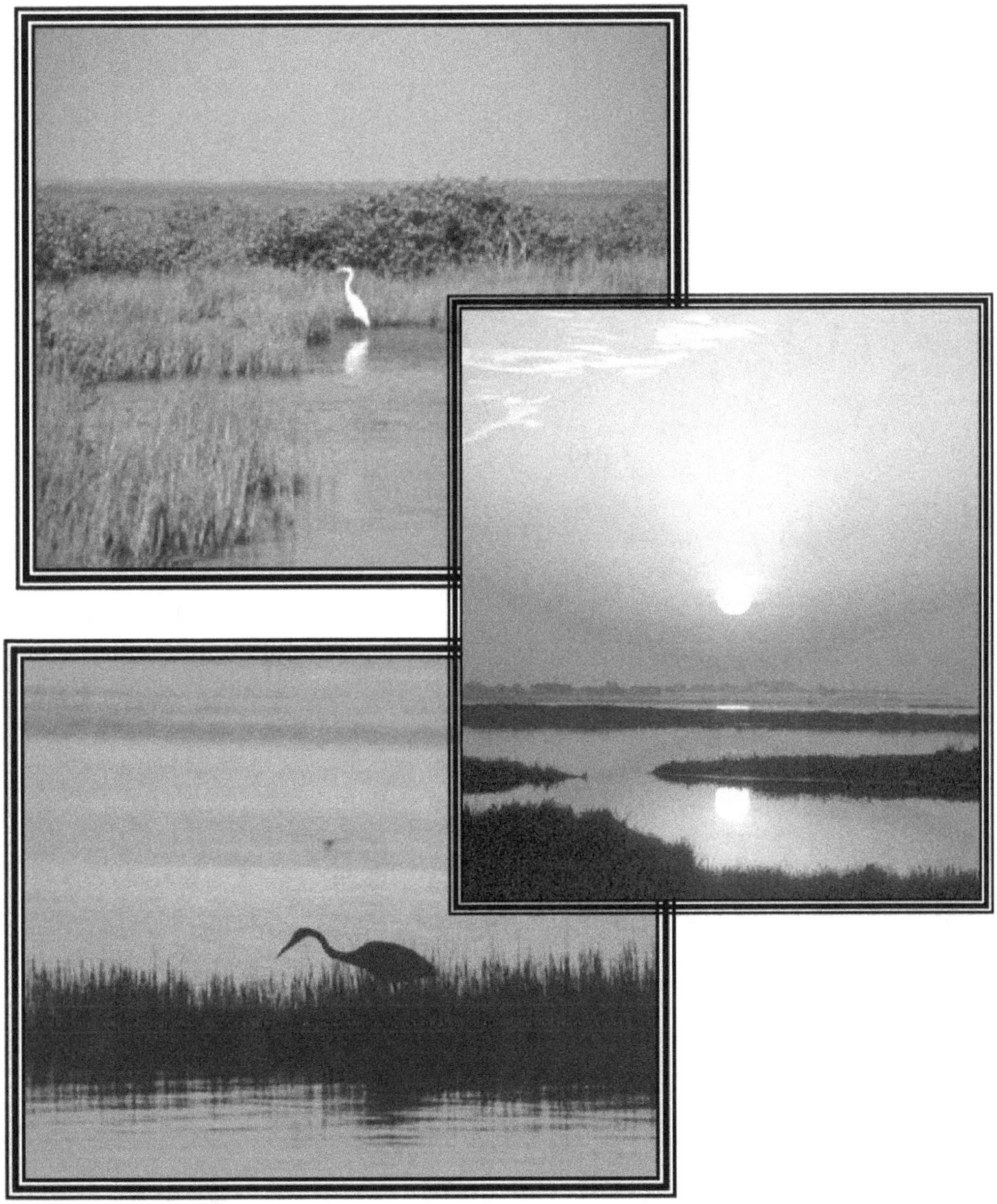

**U.S. Department of the Interior**
Minerals Management Service
Gulf of Mexico OCS Region

**Cooperative Agreement
Coastal Marine Institute
Louisiana State University**

OCS Study
MMS 2002-048

Coastal Marine Institute

# Development of Bioremediation for Oil Spill Cleanup in Coastal Wetlands

Editors

Irving A. Mendelssohn
Qianxin Lin

August 2003

Prepared under MMS Contract
14-35-0001-30660-19909
by
Louisiana State University
Wetland Biogeochemistry Institute
Center for Coastal, Energy and Environmental Resources
Baton Rouge, Louisiana  70803

Published by

**U.S. Department of the Interior**
**Minerals Management Service**
**Gulf of Mexico OCS Region**

**Cooperative Agreement**
**Coastal Marine Institute**
**Louisiana State University**

**DISCLAIMER**

This report was prepared under contract between the Minerals Management Service (MMS) and Louisiana State University. This report has been technically reviewed by the MMS and approved for publication. Approval does not signify that the contents necessarily reflect the views or policies of the Service, nor does mention of trade names or commercial products constitute endorsement or recommendation for use. It is, however, exempt from review and compliance with MMS editorial standards.

**REPORT AVAILABILITY**

Extra copies of this report may be obtained from the Public Information Office (MS 5034) at the following address:

U.S. Department of the Interior
Minerals Management Service
Gulf of Mexico OCS Region
Public Information Office (MS 5034)
1201 Elmwood Park Boulevard
New Orleans, Louisiana 70123-2394

Telephone Number: (504) 736-2519
1-800-200-GULF

**CITATION**

Suggested citation:

Mendelssohn, I.A. and L. Oianxin (ed.). 2003. The development of bioremediation for oil spill cleanup in coastal wetlands. U.S. Dept. of the Interior, Minerals Management Service, Gulf of Mexico OCS Region, New Orleans, LA. OCS Study MMS 2002-048. 84 pp.

# CONTRIBUTING AUTHORS

Irving A. Mendelssohn, Editor
Wetland Biogeochemistry Institute
School of the Coast and Environment
Louisiana State University

Nazan Atilla
Louisiana Universities Marine Consortium
8124 Highway 56
Environment
Chauvin, Louisiana

Karolien Debusschere
Coastal Environments, Inc.
1260 Main Street
Baton Rouge, Louisiana

M. Scott Miles
Institute for Environmental Studies
School of the Coast and Environment
Louisiana State University

Ralph J. Portier
Institute for Environmental Studies
School of the Coast and Environment
Louisiana State University

Pauline O. Roberts
Institute for Environmental Studies
School of the Coast and Environment
Louisiana State University

Qianzin Lin, Co-editor
Wetland Biogeochemistry Institute
School of the Coast and Environment
Louisiana State University

Charles B. Henry, Jr.
Institute for Environmental Studies
School of the Coast and
Louisiana State University

Edward B. Overton
Institute for Environmental Studies
School of the Coast and Environment
Louisiana State University

Nancy N. Rabalais
Louisiana Universities Marine Consortium
8124 Highway 56
Chauvin, Louisiana

Maud M. Walsh
Institute for Environmental Studies
School of the Coast and Environment
Louisiana State University

# ACKNOWLEDGMENTS

This project was supported by Minerals Management Service (MMS), US Department of the Interior (Contract No. 1435-0001-30660 /19909) and Exxon Company, USA. We thank Michele Young of Baton Rouge Refinery of Exxon for the Louisiana crude oil; Randy Drake of Polybac for Petrobac; Brain Birrenkott of Grace Sierra for Osmocote; FMC Corp. for PermeOx; and Paul Frederick of Exxon and Pat Roscigno of MMS for their invaluable counsel throughout this research.

**TABLE OF CONTENTS**

**FIGURES**

**TABLES**

# EXECUTIVE SUMMARY

Although bioremediation for oil spill cleanup has received considerable attention in recent years, its satisfactory use in the cleanup of oil spills in the wetland environment is still questionable and generally untested. We have conducted a multi-disciplinary experimental program to evaluate the use of various bioremediation products, including microbial seeding, inorganic fertilizer, and soil oxidant, as a means of enhancing oil biodegradation in coastal salt marshes. The overall goal was to determine the potential for oil bioremediation in coastal marshes. The specific objectives of this research were to determine (1) the toxicity and ecological safety of some common biodegradation agents, (2) the effect of these bioremediation agents on crude oil degradation under the most common marsh inundation environments, (3) the effect of biostimulants on crude oil degradation as a function of soil texture, and (4) the comparative efficacy of bioremediation and phytoremediation of oil. Chapters 1 through 4 address the above objectives.

The experiment described in Chapter 1 was designed to determine the toxicity and ecological safety of common biodegradation agents. In the greenhouse, the following bioremediation treatments were applied to salt marsh sods with intact *Spartina alterniflora*: (1) fertilizer, (2) microbial seeding, and (3) no bioremediation agent addition (control). The experimental design was a randomized block with a 3 x 2 factorial treatment arrangement (the three bioremediation types mentioned above and two oil dosage levels (oiled with 1 $L/m^2$ and no oil addition)). The results of experiment 1 indicated that all bioremediation agents used in this research, including microbial seeding and inorganic fertilizer, were not toxic to plants, microbes, and infauna animals in a salt marsh. The bioremediation agents did not adversely impact the dominant marsh macrophyte, *Spartina alterniflora*. Microbial seeding did not significantly affect the photosynthetic rate, plant stem density, leaf elongation rate, and aboveground biomass of *S. alterniflora*. However, inorganic fertilizer significantly enhanced these variables. Oil application had no significant effect on plant growth. Furthermore, bioremediation agents did not adversely affect various microbial populations, such as microbial heterotrophic populations, fungi, petroleum-utilizing populations, and overall microbial biomass. However, fertilization significantly increased soil respiration, but microbial seeding had no significant effect on soil respiration. Bioremediation agents did not adversely affect various infauna animals such as macrofauna and meiofauna. There were no significant differences in bioremediation agent treatments for either number of individuals or number of species for macrofauna and meiofauna. Gas chromatography-mass spectrometry indicated that both reduced crude oil used in this experiment and laboratory weathered crude oil appear to be acceptable since they contain a wide range of middle distillate normal hydrocarbons. Overall, the bioremediation agents used in this experiment are safe to marsh communities.

Experiment 2, which is described in Chapter 2, was designed to determine the effect of bioremediation agents on oil degradation and biotic response under drained and flooded conditions in marsh mesocosms. In the greenhouse, the following bioremediation treatments were applied to salt marsh sods with intact *Spartina alterniflora*: (1) fertilizer, (2) microbial seeding, (3) oxidant plus fertilizer, and (4) no bioremediation agent addition (control). The experimental design was a randomized block with a 4 x 2 factorial treatment arrangement. The four bioremediation types mentioned above and two inundation regimes (flooded with 3 cm of standing water and drained with the water table 10 cm below the soil surface) were included in this experiment. Reduced crude oil was applied to the surface at the rate of 2 $L/m^2$. The bioremediation agents were applied to the marsh sod surface. Fertilizer application enhanced plant growth with significantly higher photosynthetic rates, stem growth rates, and aboveground biomass of *S. alterniflora*, but microbial seeding application did not affect these variables compared to the control. Oil application and inundation regime did not have a differential effect on *S. alterniflora*. Bioremediation with a soil oxidant combined with fertilizer significantly increased interstitial phosphorus concentration, soil respiration, soil heterotrophic microbial populations, oil-degrading microbial populations, and degradation rate of alkane and aromatic hydrocarbons, especially in the drained conditions. However, the role of the soil oxidant needs further study because the soil oxidant treatment also contained extra $KH_2PO_4$ to buffer a high pH value created by the oxidant. Fertilizer application also significantly increased plant and soil variables and oil degradation. Microbial seeding did not significantly affect soil microbes or oil degradation. Oil degradation was greater in the drained condition than in the flooded condition.

Chapter 3 compares three major categories of bioremediation agents, fertilizer, microbial seeding and soil oxidant, as a means of enhancing oil biodegradation in coastal mineral and sandy marsh substrates under controlled greenhouse conditions. Artificially weathered south Louisiana crude oil was applied to sods of marsh (soil and vegetation intact) at the rate of 2 $L/m^2$. Four months after the bioremediation treatment, fertilizer application enhanced marsh plant growth, soil microbial populations, and oil biodegradation rate. Live aboveground biomass of *S. alterniflora* with fertilizer application was higher than that without fertilizer. Fertilizer significantly increased soil microbial respiration rates and the population of heterotrophic bacteria, indicating an enhanced oil biodegradation potential. Bioremediation with fertilizer significantly reduced total targeted normal hydrocarbons (TTNH) and total targeted aromatic hydrocarbons (TTAH) remaining in the soil, with concentrations of 82% and 48%, respectively, lower than those in the treatments without fertilizer. TTNH/hopane and TTAH/hopane showed similar scales of reduction, further demonstrating the enhancement of oil biodegradation by fertilization. However, soil type did not affect oil bioremediation; the extent of fertilizer-enhanced oil biodegradation was similar for sandy and mineral marsh types. Furthermore, microbial seeding and soil oxidant application had no positive effects on the variables mentioned above under the present experimental conditions. These results support the conclusion that bioremediation with inorganic nutrient additions is a promising methodology for promoting oil spill cleanup in coastal wetlands.

Chapter 4 compares the effect of phytoremediation and bioremediation on oil degradation. In the greenhouse, the following treatments were applied to the experimental units: (1) phytoremediation with *Spartina alterniflora* or without, (2) three nitrogen levels, and (3) two phosphorus level. The experimental design was a randomized block with a 2 x 3 x 2 factorial treatment arrangement. Six months after the treatments, both nitrogen and phosphorus application significantly enhanced plant growth with higher photosynthetic rate, stem density, and above- and below-ground biomass. Phytoremediation by the salt marsh plant *S. alterniflora* significantly increased soil redox potential, indicating a more oxidized soil environment that may enhance aerobic oil degradation. Phytoremediation by *S. alterniflora* enhanced oil degradation. Concentrations of residual alkane (TTNH) were significantly lower in the treatment receiving *S. alterniflora* than without phytoremediation. In addition, concentrations of residual aromatic hydrocarbons (TTAH) were significantly lower in the treatment receiving *S. alterniflora* compared to the treatment without *S. alterniflora*, and were lowest in the treatment receiving *S. alterniflora* and high doses of nitrogen. Thus, nitrogen addition enhanced the efficacy of phytoremediation on the degradation of aromatic hydrocarbons. However, bioremediation by nitrogen and phosphorus additions did not significantly affect residual oil concentration compared to no fertilizer additions in the absence of *S. alterniflora*. Concentrations of residual alkane and aromatic hydrocarbons were not significantly different between nitrogen and phosphorus treatments when *S. alterniflora* was absent in the experimental units.

# INTRODUCTION

The northern Gulf Coast of the United States is a region of intense oil exploration, production, transmission, and refining. Consequently, coastal states, such as Louisiana, are subject to oil spills resulting from shipping accidents, production-related incidents, and pipeline ruptures. Since these incidents often occur in the nearshore environment, coastal salt marshes are frequently the first wetland habitat to be subjected to the oil. As a result, a large number of investigations have documented the effect of petroleum hydrocarbon spills on the dominant salt marsh plant species, especially *Spartina alterniflora* (Hershner and Lake 1980; Lee *et al.* 1981; Alexander and Webb 1983; Ferrell *et al.* 1984; Mendelssohn *et al.* 1990; Lin and Mendelssohn 1996 and others). In addition, some investigators (DeLaune *et al.* 1984; Mendelssohn *et al.* 1993; Lin *et al.* 1999a) have evaluated the impact of oil cleanup procedures in salt marshes. Not only can petroleum hydrocarbons have a detrimental impact on coastal marshes, but, additionally, the cleanup of the oil from these highly sensitive environments is often more damaging than the oil itself. Hence, it is important to develop less intrusive oil spill cleanup procedures that exert little to no impact on wetland ecosystems.

Bioremediation is the act of adding materials to contaminated environments, such as oil spill sites, to cause an acceleration of the natural biodegradation process (U.S. Congress 1991). It is a promising means by which oil released into salt marshes, as well as other wetland types, can be removed with little impact to the habitat. Bacteria, cultured and selected for high rates of oil degradation, and fertilizers, which enhance native microbial activity, are two types of bioremediation products that can be added to oil-contaminated wetlands.

Inorganic fertilizer, which enhances native microbial activity, is one of the most common bioremediation agents applied to oil contaminated wetlands. A number of studies have demonstrated the potential for enhanced oil degradation as a result of bioremediation, especially through nutrient additions (Lee and Levy 1987; Tabak *et al.* 1991; Safferman 1991; Lee and Levy 1991; Bragg *et al.* 1993; Lee *et al.* 1993). Specifically for wetlands, Scherrer and Mille (1990) confirmed enhanced degradation of oil in a West Indies mangrove swamp after the addition of an oleophilic fertilizer. Similarly, Lee and Levy (1991) found enhanced degradation of oil, this time in salt marsh sediments, treated with inorganic nutrients. However, critical evaluations of oil bioremediation potential in wetland environments, based on oil chemical analyses that can unequivocally identify enhanced biodegradation, is sparse in the published literature.

Microbial seeding as a means of enhancing oil biodegradation, has even greater uncertainties associated with it, especially in systems such as wetlands where hydrocarbon degrading bacteria are naturally prevalent. For example, microbial seeding was used in an experimental mode to test its effectiveness in cleaning up an oil spill in a marsh (Marrow Marsh) in Galveston Bay. The reported results did not indicate that the microbial seeding significantly degraded oil at this marsh site (Mearns 1991). In a more recent investigation (Venosa *et al.* 1992), two microbial products, which exhibited enhanced biodegradation of Alaska North Slope crude oil in shaker flask tests, did not accelerate biodegradation in a field experiment conducted on an oiled beach in Prince William Sound. The high variability in the data, the highly weathered nature of the oil, and a lack of sufficient time for biodegradation were cited as possible reasons for the lack of response. Regardless of these equivocal results, many microbial products have been commercialized. If added microbes, per se, are not effective in increasing oil degradation, the high costs of microbial amendments may not be warranted. Oil response agencies, both public and private, require a critical evaluation of microbial seeding in enhancing oil biodegradation.

Soil oxidation status is another important factor influencing oil biodegradation in wetland environments. Generally, wetland soils are saturated with water and exhibit biochemically reduced soil conditions, which may limit oil degradation (Hambrick et al. 1980). Therefore, procedures that increase the oxidation status of sediments may favor bioremediation (Lin and Mendelssohn 1997). The use of soil oxidants to increase oil biodegradation in the wetland environment has received little attention (McKee and Mendelssohn 1995).

Finally, the ecological impacts of application of these bioremediation agents to wetland environments, if any, must be identified before a large scale bioremediation is conducted.

This report describes the results from a multi-disciplinary, multi-investigator research program initiated to address the question: Is bioremediation, via fertilization, microbial seeding or soil oxidant, an effective and ecologically safe means of oil spill cleanup in coastal wetlands?

## Overall Goal and Objectives

The overall goal of the research was to determine the potential use of bioremediation as an oil-spill cleanup technique in wetlands. The specific objectives of this study were to
  (1) determine the potential toxicity and ecological impacts, if any, of bioremediation agents on wetlands,
  (2) determine the effectiveness of bioremediation by application of fertilizer, microbial seeding, or soil oxidant, singly or in combination, on oil degradation,
  (3) determine the bioremediation effectiveness under different marsh inundation conditions,
  (4) determine the effectiveness of bioremediation of oil under different marsh types,
  (5) identify the role of nitrogen or phosphorus, singly or in combination, in bioremediation of oil, and
  (6) separate the effectiveness of bioremediation and phytoremediation of oil.
To accomplish the preceding goal and objectives, we divided the project into four separate experiments as reported in each chapter.

## Project Organization

The effectiveness of bioremediation and its ecological safety were assessed in the experiments described below by evaluating the following: (1) petroleum hydrocarbon chemistry to identify and quantify the degree of oil biodegradation, (2) oil morphology, which is related to oil chemistry, as an inexpensive means of evaluating oil biodegradation, (3) soil microbial response to determine the effect of the bioremediation products on the microbial communities that are performing the oil biodegradation, (4) soil chemistry to determine the effect of the bioremediation products on those factors that limit the growth of microbes and plants (e.g. nutrients, soil reducing conditions and soil toxins), (5) plant response to evaluate the combined effects of the oil and products on plant components of the marsh system, and (6) infaunal response to evaluate the combined effects of the oil and products on animal components of the marsh system.

### Chapter 1
The first experiment was designed to determine the potential toxicity and ecological impacts, if any, of bioremediation agents on wetland plants, infaunal animals, and microbial communities. This experiment is required to ensure that the product loading rates suggested by the manufacturer are not toxic to wetland plants and estuarine animals. Only products on the National Contingency Plan (NCP) list, with defined maximum loading rates, were used in this study.

### Chapter 2
The second experiment was designed (a) to evaluate the effectiveness of bioremediation by application of fertilizer, microbial seeding, or soil oxidant on oil degradation and (b) to determine the bioremediation effectiveness under different marsh inundation conditions. Since large-scale field demonstration projects are exceedingly expensive to initiate and complete, it is prudent to first evaluate bioremediation in smaller and less complicated greenhouse marsh-mesocosm experiments before scaling-up to field demonstration trials.

### Chapter 3
The third experiment was designed (a) to determine the effectiveness of bioremediation by application of fertilizer, microbial seeding, and soil oxidant, singly and in combination, on oil degradation and (b) to determine the effectiveness of bioremediation of oil for different marsh types. Salt marsh soils, depending on their texture and specific microbial communities, may exhibit different capacities for bioremediation, which must be quantified to access the variability in bioremediation potential of salt marshes.

### Chapter 4
The fourth experiment was designed (a) to identify the role of nitrogen and phosphorus, singly and in combination, in bioremediation of oil and (b) to identify the relative effectiveness of bioremediation and phytoremediation of oil.

# CHAPTER 1

## AN INVESTIGATION OF THE POTENTIAL TOXICITY
## OF BIOREMEDIATION AGENTS IN WETLAND MESOCOSMS

by Irving A. Mendelssohn, Qianxin Lin, and Charles B. Henry, Edward B. Overton,
Ralph J. Portier, Nazan Atilla, Nancy N. Rabalais, Pauline O. Roberts, and Maud M. Walsh

Efficacy and success of bioremediation of oil by adding materials to contaminated environments to accelerate the biodegradation process depend on the extent of contaminant removal and on the ecological safety of the bioremediation agents. Thus, bioremediation agents for oil spill cleanup must not negatively impact wetland structure and function. Generally, common bioremediation agents such as inorganic fertilizer and selected microbial agents are relatively safe to environments. Microbial inocula are selected from natural soils that have the potential for enhancing oil degradation. Nitrogen and phosphorus fertilizers are widely used in agriculture to enhance the growth of crops and other plants. However, little information is available concerning the impact of bioremediation agents on the biotic components of wetlands.

The microbial community is an important wetland component in affecting organic matter decomposition and nutrient transformations, and it is particularly important in the carbon-rich salt marsh environments (Hood and Meyers 1978). Microbial degradation is one of the most important processes to cleanup organic contaminants (Bragg et al. 1993). Many microbial products have been commercialized to enhance bioremediation, especially for oil degradation. However, microbial seeding as a means of enhancing oil biodegradation has considerable uncertainties because in areas commonly exposed to a certain contaminant, such as oil, there usually exists populations of microorganisms that is well-adapted to tolerating and/or degrading the contaminant. In addition, soil fertility may affect microbial community. A number of studies (Thirukkumaran and Parkinson 2000; Arnebrant et al. 1996; Nohrstedt et al. 1989) have found that addition of ammonium nitrate, ammonium sulfate, and urea suppressed soil microbial respiration. However, increased soil microbial respiration by the addition of urea and ammonium nitrate was also noted in short term incubations (Roberge 1976; Thirukkumaran and Parkinson 2000). Effects of phosphorus fertilizer on soil microbes have also been reported as negative, neutral, or positive (Thirukkumaran and Parkinson 2000; Amador and Jones 1993). The tracking of various components of the microbial community is important in predicting the overall response of the ecosystem. The enumeration of these populations provides a direct measure of microbial response.

Studies of the effects of chemical discharges and oil spills have also focused on the benthos because organisms living or feeding at the sediment-water interface, such as meiofauna and macrofauna, may be exposed to particularly high concentrations of contaminants. Typical responses of benthic communities to the addition of toxic materials from chemical discharges or spills may include the reduction or elimination of species or individuals (Boesch and Rabalais 1989; Rabalais et al. 1992) or increases in populations of opportunistic species and reduction in species diversity (Addy et al. 1984; Boesch and Rabalais 1989; Nance 1991). The benthos is composed of macrobenthos, meiobenthos, and microbenthos, operationally defined by size and, often, taxonomic and functional groups (e.g., life history stage). However, few studies have focused on both, probably due to the high labor requirements for thorough benthic community analyses in these groups, and limitations of taxonomic expertise to select groups. Each component provides important information with regards to environmental impacts (Sanders et al. 1980; Hampson and Moul 1978; Lee et al. 1981; Boucher 1980; Fricke et al. 1981; Wornald, 1976; Holt et al. 1978; Spies 1987).

Plants are the important wetland primary producers providing food and habitat for consumer and decomposer. Environmental change may influence productivity and alter wetland structure and function. Oil spills may detrimentally affect wetland plants (Ferrell et al. 1984; Alexander and Webb 1987; Mendelssohn et al. 1990, Lin and Mendelssohn 1996) or do little plant damage (Burk 1977; Hershner and Moore 1977; Li et al. 1990, Lin and Mendelssohn 1996), depending upon such things as oil type, oil amount or plant species. Fertilization, such as application of nitrogen and phosphorus, generally increases marsh plant growth (Wilsey et al. 1992; Lin and Mendelssohn 1998a; Lin et al. 1999b). However, little information is available on the effects of microbial seeding on wetland plants since most of microbial inoculation studies focus on the response of the microbial community.

3

The objectives of this study were to determine if the bioremediation agents, inorganic fertilizer and a commercial microbial product, generate adverse impacts to wetland plants, infaunal animals, and microbial communities. We specifically asked the question: Can bioremediation be used for oil spill cleanup without causing negative impacts to wetland structure and function?

## Materials and Methods

### Experimental Design

Sods of marsh (soil and vegetation intact), approximately 28 cm in diameter (0.06 $m^2$) and 30 cm deep, were collected from the inland zone (approximately 5 m from the creekbank natural levee) of a *Spartina alterniflora*-dominated salt marsh located west of Cocodrie, Louisiana, and used as the experimental units. Inland sods were chosen because the inland zone comprises the largest aerial extent of most salt marshes. We recognize that soil types will likely influence bioremediation, and, thus, this factor will be examined in future research. *Spartina alterniflora* is the dominant inter-tidal salt marsh grass along the Atlantic and Gulf Coasts of the United States, and thus results from this study generally will be applicable to many other salt marshes.

In the greenhouse, the following treatments were randomly assigned to the collected sods: (1) fertilizer product, (2) microbial seeding agent, and (3) no bioremediation agent addition (control). The experimental design was a randomized block with a 3 x 2 factorial treatment arrangement (three bioremediation types mentioned above and two oil dosage levels: oiled with 1 $L/m^2$ and no oil addition as a control). Each treatment combination was replicated 5 times for a total of 30 marsh sods.

### Experimental Procedures

A reduced crude (with nC-13 and below absent) was added to the surface water of the mesocosms at a dose of 1 $L/m^2$ (1 mm of oil thickness) of 15 experimental units (marsh sods in 28 cm x 30 cm buckets fitted with water level controls). An additional 15 experimental units without oil served as controls. The reduced crude simulated the kind of oil that might impact a marsh after the oil had been spilled in open water and subsequently transported into the salt marsh by winds or tides. After the applied oil was evenly spread over the surface water in the buckets, the water was drained from the bottom of the buckets to allow the oil to come in contact with and penetrate the soil of each sod. The bioremediation products utilized were those proven to be most successful in enhancing oil biodegradation from marsh sediment-microcosm experiments performed by Ms. Sara McMillen of Exxon Production Research, Houston, Texas, as part of this project. This work employed both respirometry and oil chemistry (GC-FID) to identify enhanced oil biodegradation. The results indicated that Customblen, a fertilizer product used during the Valdez Spill and Petrobac, a microbial product, show promise as bioremediation agents (personal communication, Sara McMillen, Exxon Production Research). Thus, we used these two products in the present experiment.

The Customblen used in this study contained 28% N and 8% P as ammonium nitrate, calcium phosphate and ammonium phosphate (Bragg *et al.* 1992). Petrobac contained microbes, without any fertilizer, selected for hydrocarbon degradation in a saline medium (personal communicatiaon, R. Drake, Polybac Corp.). The bioremediation treatments (fertilizer, microbial seeding and control) were applied to both oiled and unoiled marsh sods. The bioremediation agents were applied to the soil surface in a manner similar to that during a field application and following the manufacturer's specifications (Customblen: 93 $g/m^2$; Petrobac: 0.833 $L/m^2$ of inoculum (46 g of Petrobac/ L of de-ionized water)). The sod-mesocosms were kept moist, but drained by maintaining an average water level at 5 cm below the soil surface. Water levels were allowed to fluctuate due to evapo-transpiration, but they were re-watered daily to 5 cm below the soil surface to maintain relatively constant salinity.

Statistical analysis was conducted with the SAS system (SAS 1990). General Linear Model (GLM) was used to test for statistically significant differences ($P<0.05$) among the treatments, and Duncan's multiple range test was used to determine significant differences among the main factors. Treatment-level combination differences, if interactions of main factors were significant, were tested with least square means.

**Methods**

<u>Plant Response</u>

*Photosynthetic Rate.*  Leaf photosynthetic rate was measured to indicate plant growth status.  A portable photosynthesis system, including an infrared gas analyzer (IRGA) (The Analytical Development Co. Ltd, (ADC) model LCA-2), an ADC air flow control unit, and an ADC Parkinson leaf chamber, was used.  Sample air, taken 5 m aboveground to obtain relatively stable $CO_2$ concentrations, was led through the ADC air flow control unit at a flow rate of 5 ml/s during photosynthetic rate measurements.  Measurements were conducted at a quantum flux density of 2000 $\mu mol/m^2/s^1$ provided by a Kodak projector lamp.  An intact, attached and fully expanded young leaf was enclosed in the leaf chamber and the difference in $CO_2$ concentration and humidity between inlet and outlet air was measured.  Photosynthetic rate ($CO_2$ exchange) was calculated in accordance with von Caemmerer and Farquhar (1981) and expressed as $\mu mol\ CO_2/m^2/s$.

*Plant Stem Density.*  Plant stem density was measured by direct counting of stem number in each experimental unit and expressed as the number of stems per pot.

*Average and Maximum Shoot Height.*  The average shoot height and maximum shoot height of the transplants were measured to the nearest centimeter.

*Aboveground Biomass of Dominant Marsh Plants.*  Plant aboveground biomass was analyzed at the end of a four-month experimental period to determine the effect of product addition on plant growth.  Plant aboveground material was clipped at the soil surface.  Live and dead components were separated, dried in an oven at 65°C to constant weight, and weighed.

<u>Soil Response</u>

*Soil Respiration Rate.*  *In-situ* measurements of soil respiration rate, an indicator of soil microbial activity, were made with an infra-red gas analyzer (IRGA) by measuring carbon dioxide production from the soil.  A PVC chamber (4 cm in diameter and 8 cm in height) with one open end was equipped with an inlet and an outlet for air flow through the chamber.  The open end of the chamber was inserted into the soil 4 cm below the soil surface.  An air flow rate through the chamber was held constant at 300 ml per minute by an ADC mass flow controller.  The respiratory $CO_2$ produced from the soil resulted in a difference in $CO_2$ concentration between inlet and outlet that was measured by an ADC infra-red gas analyzer.  Soil respiration was calculated based on the $CO_2$ exchange rate from the soil per unit surface area.

*Soil Redox Potential .*  Soil redox potentials at 2 and 10 cm depths were determined with bright platinum electrodes and a calomel reference electrode.  Readings were taken with a portable pH/mV digital meter. The potential of a calomel reference electrode (+244 mV) was added to each value to calculate Eh (Patrick et al. 1996).

*Soil Nutrient Concentrations.*  Interstitial water samples were withdrawn from soil sods with a simple apparatus as described by McKee et al. (1988).  This consisted of a small diameter (3 mm inside diameter) rigid plastic tube, containing numerous holes (ca. 0.5 mm diameter) covered with 3 to 4 layers of cheesecloth, connected to a 30 ml syringe.  The collected interstitial water was filtered through a 0.45-syringe filter.  Inorganic nutrients in the filtered interstitial water were analyzed to determine the effect of product application on soil fertility and other variables.  Ammonium-nitrogen ($NH_4$) and nitrate-nitrogen ($NO_3 + NO_2$) were analyzed with an auto-analyzer. Total inorganic nitrogen was determined as the sum of $NH_4$, $NO_3$, and $NO_2$-nitrogen concentrations.  Phosphorus and potassium concentrations in the interstitial water were analyzed with ICP (inductively coupled argon-plasma emission spectrometer).

*Interstitial pH and Salinity.*  Interstitial water samples were withdrawn from soil sods as described below. Interstitial pH was measured with a digital pH meter (Model 420A, Orion) and interstitial salinity was measured with a salt refractometer.

## Microbial Response

Determining the response of the salt marsh microbial component of the ecosystem was accomplished by measuring general microbial heterotrophic populations, cellulose-utilizing populations, chitin-utilizing populations, yeast and fungi, petroleum-utilizing populations, and overall microbial biomass. Samples were collected at the termination of the experiment for the Microtox toxicity assay.

Samples of marsh soil were collected with a 5 cc syringe with the end cut off and the remaining edge sharpened to facilitate penetration into the soil. Samples for microbial analysis were taken from the top 3 cm in two locations in the marsh sod for each sampling episode. The two samples were mixed to form a composite sample. Samples were taken from each mesocosm on days 3, 14, 28, and 90. On day 90, 100 gm of soil to a depth of the top 5 cm were collected from each mesocosm for Microtox analysis. General microbial populations and several key components were tracked using plate count methods on a variety of selective agars. Nutrient agar (Difco) was used to grow general heterotrophic populations. Chitin agar was made according to modifications of recipes in Hood and Meyers (1978) and Scherbarth (1984). Martin's agar (Martin, 1950) was used for detection for yeast and filamentous fungi and Jensen's agar (Jensen 1930), modified by the addition of cellulose, for the enumeration of cellulose-degrading bacteria and actinomycetes. A minimal salts agar to which 50 ppm naphthalene and 50 ppm cresol were added as the sole carbon source was used for the selective culturing of petroleum-degrading organisms. General microbial biomass was measured using the adenosine triphosphate method (Bianchini et al. 1988). All microbial population measurements and ATP values are reported per gram dry weight. The Microtox assay was performed on the samples from Day 90; the samples were centrifuged to separate the interstitial water, and the water was analyzed according to the procedure outlined for toxicity measurements on hazardous waste land treatment demonstrations (USEPA 1984).

## Infaunal Response

*Macroinfauna.* Because of the size of the macroinfaunal cores (7.6 cm diameter), macroinfaunal samples were collected only at the termination of the experiment. A 7.6-cm diameter area was marked in each mesocosm at the beginning of the experiment to be left intact for eventual macroinfaunal sampling. Five additional marsh sods not used in the experiment were sampled for macroinfauna at the beginning of the experiment to determine the pre-treatment status of the community. Macroinfauna cores were taken to a depth of 10 cm, preserved in 10% buffered formalin stained with Rose Bengal, and transported to the laboratory at Louisiana Universities Marine Consortium (LUMCON)

Within 48 hours, the formalin in the benthic samples was decanted over a 0.5-mm sieve, the sample rinsed with water, and the sample returned to 75% ethanol for storage until analysis. Organisms were sorted in water from gridded dishes under a dissecting microscope. The debris from a sample was rechecked for any missed organisms. If any were found, the sample was resorted. Organisms were counted and identified to the lowest possible taxon. Because of the difficulty in identification of certain marsh organisms, taxonomy for oligochaetes and insect larvae were less specific than for other macroinfauna, (e.g., polychaetes, bivalves, gastropods, pericaridean crustaceans).

*Meiofauna.* A series of meiofauna collections was taken during the experiment. Fifteen meiofauna cores (2.54 cm diameter) were taken from the salt marsh where the cores were collected to compare to cores taken from 9-week acclimated sods in the greenhouse and to determine the effects of the acclimation period on the meiofauna community.

Samples were collected from pre-treatment mesocosms to determine where the majority of the meiofauna were distributed vertically in a core. Splits of 2.54-cm diameter cores were made at 0-1, 1-2, 2-3, and 3-4 cm on a precision core extruder. We determined that most of the meiofauna were in the upper 3 cm of the cores (see Results); this protocol was used for the remainder of the experiment. At the same time the macroinfauna pre-treatment samples were collected, three replicates from each of five mesocosms were sampled for meiofauna.

For the experiment, meiofauna were collected with a bulk density coring device (2.3 cm diameter) to a depth of 3 cm at days 0 and 1, weeks 2, 4, and 12. The majority of meiofaunal organisms (74-99%) were distributed in the upper 3 cm of the sediment. All cores were taken between *Spartina* culms. When a meiofauna core was removed from a sod, a core from a similarly treated spare sod was used to replace it. The replaced core was marked, and the area was not re-sampled on subsequent days.

Meiofauna samples were preserved in 10% formalin stained with Rose Bengal. The samples were sieved through two different mesh sizes: 500 μm to retain the root mass and 63 μm to retain the meiofauna. After sieving, Ludox AM centrifugation was used to extract the meiofauna. The supernatant was examined for organisms. The pellet from the centrifuge tube was examined to see if the extraction method was efficient. Nematodes, copepods, copepod nauplii and oligochaetes were counted under a dissection microscope. Only copepods were preserved for further identification. Numbers per core were converted to numbers per 10 $cm^2$.

All meiofauna samples contained dense root mass. To remove the mass, samples were sieved through a 500-μm mesh sieve and examined for any retained larger meiofauna, such as oligochaetes. Few, if any, were observed, and we concluded that most meiofauna passed through the 500-μm sieve and were retained on the 63-μm sieve. The meiofauna retained on the 63-μm sieve were extracted with Ludox AM by centrifugation. Meiofauna were identified to major taxa, which included nematodes, harpacticoid copepods, oligochaetes, copepod nauplii and miscellaneous organisms. Miscellaneous organisms included some isopods, polychaetes and some other groups of benthic meiofauna. The harpacticoid copepod adults were identified to family or species.

Abundances were calculated as number of organisms per 10 $cm^2$. The copepod:nematode ratio was determined rather than the standard nematode:copepod ratio because the number of copepods was frequently zero. The ratio was multiplied by 1000 for plotting results.

Residual Oil Chemistry in the Soil.

The top five cm of soil from each sod was collected with the same technique as for the microbial samples, thoroughly homogenized, and extracted using a modified EPA method 3550. Approximately 20 grams of wet sediment were extracted using dichloromethane and sodium sulfate as a chemical drying agent (Venosa et al. 1996; Sauer and Boehm 1991; Henry and Overton 1993; Henry et al. 1993), then reduced to a final volume of 10 ml. A field treatment composite was then analyzed by gas chromatography-mass spectrometry (GC/MS) operated in the Selective Ion Monitoring (SIM) mode to characterize compositional changes in targeted normal hydrocarbons (NH) and aromatic hydrocarbons (AH). Although these targeted AH generally represent less than 5% of the bulk oil composition, they are essential to characterize the petroleum source, identify potential biological effects, determine exposure pathways, and monitor weathering trends and degradation of the oil (Sauer and Boehm 1991, Roques et al. 1994). The targeted aromatic hydrocarbons are listed in Table 1.

**Results**

Responses of *Spartina alterniflora*

The effect of the bioremediation agents and oil on the growth response of *Spartina alterniflora* was assessed by determining plant leaf elongation rate, photosynthetic rate, stem density, and aboveground biomass. There was no adverse effect of microbial seeding on plant leaf elongation rate (Fig. 1), photosynthetic rate (Fig. 2), relative growth rate based on plant stem density and cumulative shoot height (Fig. 3), and live and total plant aboveground biomass (Fig. 4). Furthermore, fertilization significantly enhanced plant growth as evidenced by higher plant leaf elongation rate (Fig. 1), photosynthetic rate (Fig. 2), relative growth rate (Fig. 3), and live and total plant aboveground biomass (Fig. 4) compared to the control. The addition of the reduced crude oil to the marsh mesocosms had no significant impact on plant response, and there was no significant interaction between bioremediation agents and the oil addition (Table 2). Thus neither the bioremediation agents nor the oil had negative impacts on the vegetation.

Table 1.  Targeted Compounds Assessed by GC/MS

| Compound | *ion* mass | Compound | *ion* mass |
|---|---|---|---|
| alkanes* (nC-10 thru nC-31) | 85 | fluoranthrene/pyrene | 202 |
| decalin* | 138 | naphthobenzothiophene | 234 |
| C-1 decalin* | 152 | C-1 pyrenes | 216 |
| C-2 decalin* | 166 | C-2 pyrenes | 230 |
| C-3 decalin* | 180 | chrysene | 228 |
| naphthalene | 128 | C-1 chrysenes | 242 |
| C-1 naphthalenes | 142 | C-2 chrysenes | 256 |
| C-2 naphthalenes | 156 | phenanthrene | 178 |
| C-3 naphthalenes | 170 | C-1 phenanthrenes | 192 |
| C-4 naphthalenes | 184 | C-2 phenanthrenes | 206 |
| fluorene | 166 | C-3 phenanthrenes | 220 |
| C-1 fluorenes | 180 | C-1 naphthobenzothiophenes | 248 |
| C-2 fluorenes | 194 | C-2 naphthobenzothiophenes | 262 |
| C-3 fluorenes | 208 | C-3 naphthobenzothiophenes | 276 |
| dibenzothiophene | 184 | benzo(b)fluoranthene | 252 |
| C-1 dibenzothiophenes | 198 | benzo(k)fluoranthene | 252 |
| C-2 dibenzothiophenes | 212 | benzo(e)pyrene | 252 |
| C-3 dibenzothiophenes | 226 | benzo(a)pyrene | 252 |
| perylene | 252 | benzo(g,h,i)perylene | 276 |
| indeno(1,2,3-cd)pyrene | 276 | hopanes (191 family)* | 191 |
| dibenzo(a,h)anthracene | 278 | sterenes (217 family)* | 217 |

Sum of these compounds excluding those identified with a * is the TTAH value.

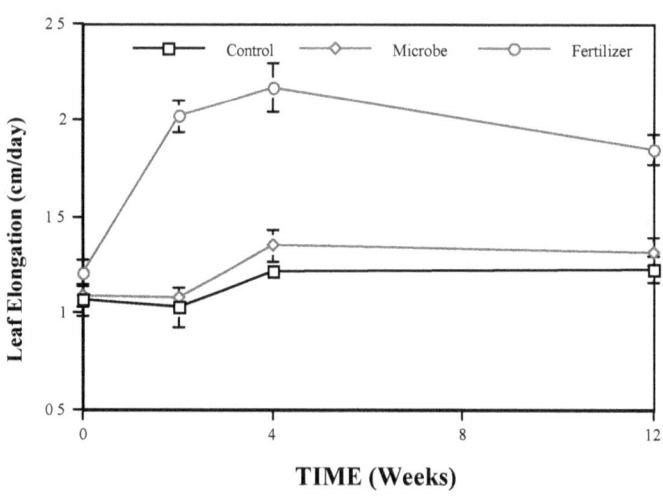

Figure 1.  Effect of bioremediation agents on leaf elongation rate of *Spartina alterniflora*. Values are means averaged over oil treatments (n=10) with standard errors.

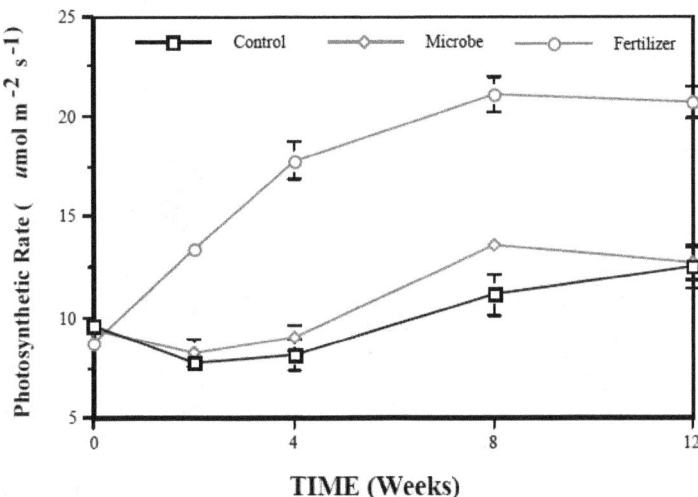

Figure 2. Effect of bioremediation agents on photosynthetic rate of *Spartina alterniflora*. Values are means averaged over oil treatments (n=10) with standard errors.

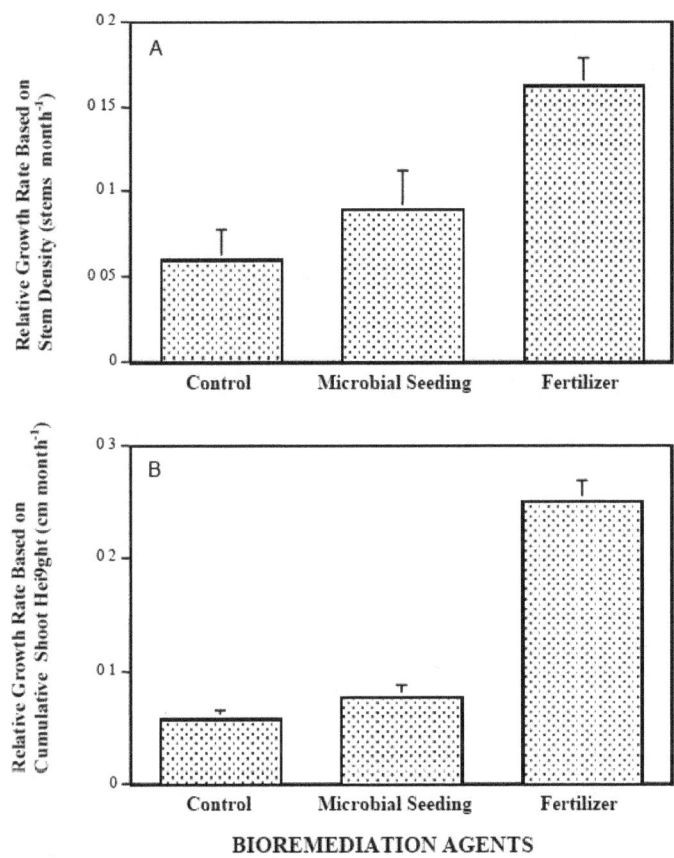

Figure 3. Effect of bioremediation agents on the relative growth based on stem density (A) and cumulative shoot height (B) of *Spartina alterniflora*. Values are means averaged over oil treatments (n=10) with standard errors.

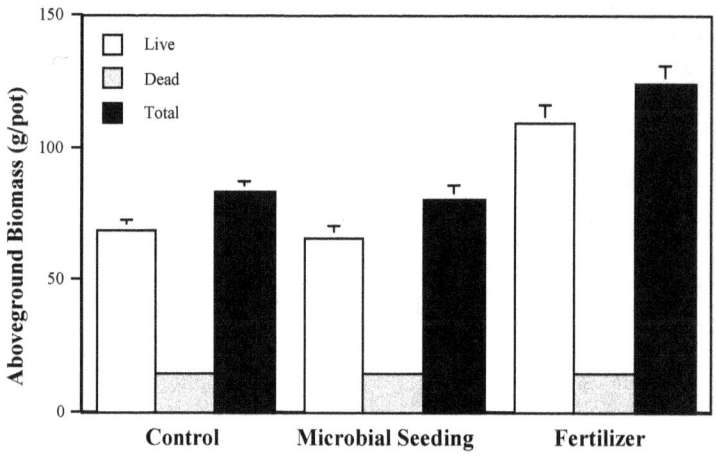

Figure 4.   Effect of bioremediation agents on aboveground biomass of *Spartina alterniflora*.  Values are means averaged over oil treatments (n=10) with standard errors.

Table 2.   Statistical Table with P-Value of Response of Marsh Plant and Soil Variables to Bioremediation Agent and Oil Application

| Variables | Bioremediation Agent | Oil | Agent * oil |
|---|---|---|---|
| Live Biomass | 0.0001 | 0.7487 | 0.6852 |
| Dead Biomass | 0.0959 | 0.9703 | 0.3807 |
| Total Biomass | 0.0001 | 0.4827 | 0.8486 |
| Stem density increase in 3 Months | 0.0021 | 0.1169 | 0.1525 |
| Cumulative height increase in 3 months | 0.0001 | 0.2317 | 0.7999 |
| Soil respiration 4 wk | 0.0056 | 0.032 | 0.5137 |
| 12 wk | 0.0003 | 0.0442 | 0.7452 |
| Leaf Elongation rate | | | |
| 2 wk | 0.0001 | 0.7541 | 0.4710 |
| 4 wk | 0.0001 | 0.5830 | 0.0889 |
| 12 wk | 0.0001 | 0.4706 | 0.0664 |
| Photosynthetic rate | | | |
| 0 wk | 0.3866 | 0.3950 | 0.4659 |
| 2 wk | 0.0001 | 0.2673 | 0.3098 |
| 4 wk | 0.0001 | 0.2956 | 0.8369 |
| 8 wk | 0.0001 | 0.5601 | 0.6226 |
| 12 wk | 0.0001 | 0.0356 | 0.2699 |

Soil physico-chemical parameters did not greatly change with the application of oil and bioremediation agents.  Interstitial pH did not significantly change with the application of bioremediation agents (Fig. 5), although the pH values at weeks 8 and 12 showed minor decreases  (0.4 pH differential) that were not likely of biological significance.

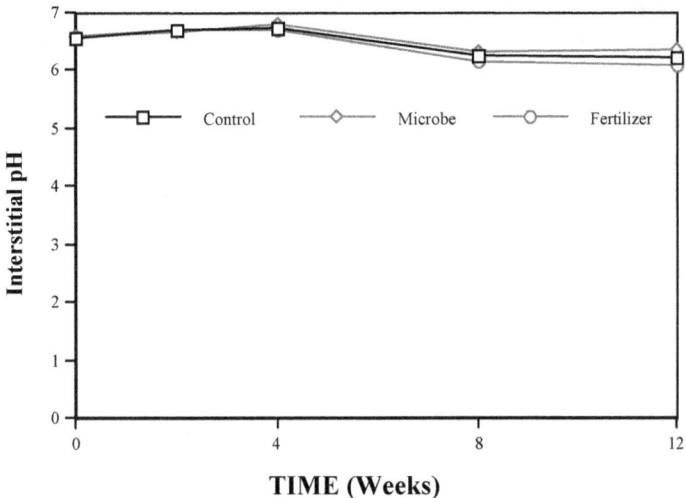

Figure 5.   Effect of bioremediation agents on interstitial pH. Values are means averaged over oil treatments (n=10) with standard errors.

The soil redox potential (Eh) at the 2 cm depth was significantly higher in the fertilizer treatment compared to control (Fig. 6). The soil redox potential at 12 cm was not significantly different with either bioremediation agent or oil (Fig. 6). Interstitial salinity was not significantly affected by either the bioremediation agents or the oil and was in the range of 10 to 11.5 parts per thousand during the 3-month experimental period (data not shown). Concentrations of interstitial sulfide, inorganic nitrogen and phosphorus measured 0, 2, 4, 8, and 12 weeks after the treatment were not significantly different with the application of either the bioremediation agents or the oil (data not shown). Overall, the applications of the bioremediation agents and the reduced oil did not adversely affect soil parameters.

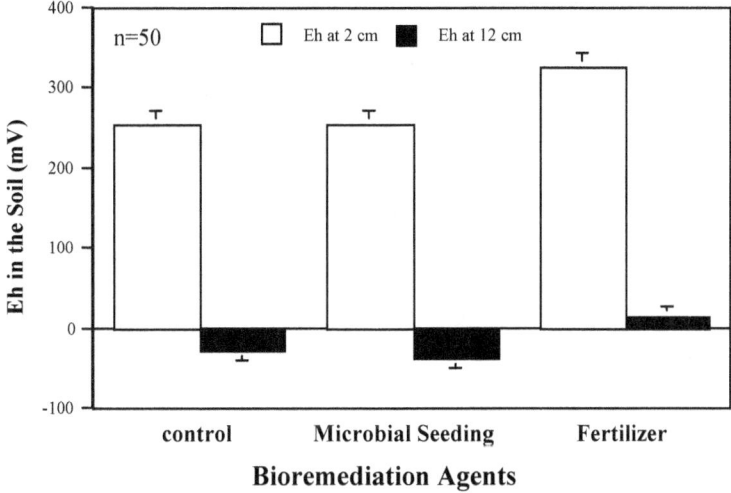

Figure 6.   Effect of bioremediation agents on soil redox potential. Values (n=50) are means averaged over oil levels and 5 repeated measurements (weeks 0, 2, 4, 8, and 12) with standard errors.

Responses of Microbial Community

In-situ soil respiration was measured to identify whether the bioremediation agents and oil affected the metabolism of the soil community. The fertilizer application had a significantly positive effect on soil respiration

11

compared to both the control and the microbial treatments (Fig. 7). Soil respiration in the microbial treatment, however, was not significantly different from that of the control, suggesting that microbial seeding had no adverse effect on the activity of the soil community.

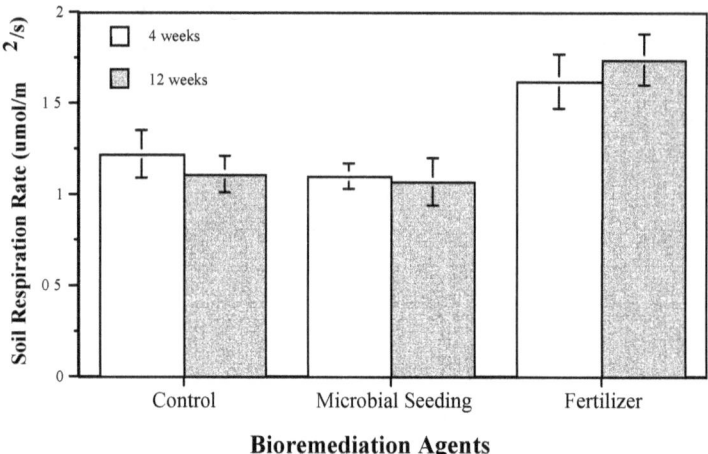

Figure 7. Effect of bioremediation agents on soil respiration rate. Values are means averaged over oil treatments (n=10) with standard errors.

A number of soil microbial components, such as the general heterotrophic microbial populations (Fig. 8), cellulose-utilizing populations (Fig. 9), chitin-utilizing populations (Fig. 10), yeast (Fig. 11), fungi (Fig. 12), petroleum-utilizing populations (Fig. 13), and overall microbial biomass (Fig. 14), were measured 3 and 28 days after bioremediation agent addition. Overall, there were no significant differences among the bioremediation agents. After three days, there were no statistically significant differences in the various microbial components (Figs. A1-1 to A1-7 in Appendix A) among the bioremediation agents and oil addition (Table 3). The short-term results suggest no acute toxicity of the bioremediation agents and oil to the general microbial populations. After 28 days, the bioremediation agents did not significantly affect the various microbial parameters (Figs. 13) except microbial ATP (Fig 14); ATP was higher in the fertilizer treatment compared to the control and the inoculated treatments (Table 3). After 28 days, oil addition adversely affected the microbial heterotrophic populations (Fig. 8), fungi (Fig. 13), petroleum-utilizing populations (Fig. 9), and overall microbial biomass (Fig. 14), but did not significantly affect cellulose-utilizing populations, chitin-utilizing populations, and yeast (Table 3). A significant interaction between bioremediation agent and oil application on ATP indicated that fertilizer enhanced ATP only in treatments without oil application (Fig. 14). Microtox analyses conducted on samples from day 90 show no significant difference in toxicity (measured as EC 50 at 15 minutes) between samples treated with either fertilizer or microbial seeding for either the oiled or the unoiled samples (Fig 15).

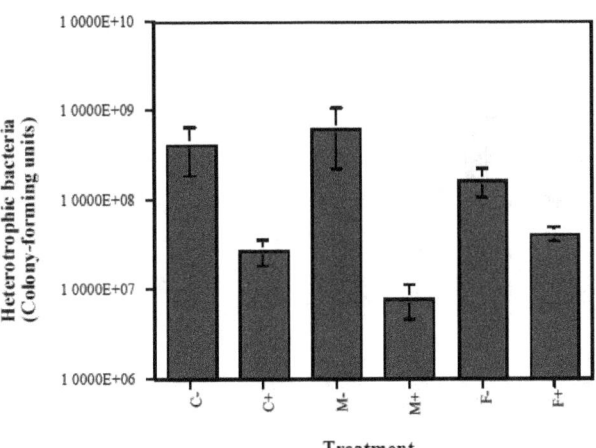

Figure 8.  Effect of bioremediation agents and oil application on heterotrophic bacteria 28 days after treatment. Values are reported in colony-forming units per gram (dry weight) of soil with standard errors. C: control; M: microbial seeding; F: fertilizer.  Plus signs indicate oiling and minus signs no oiling.

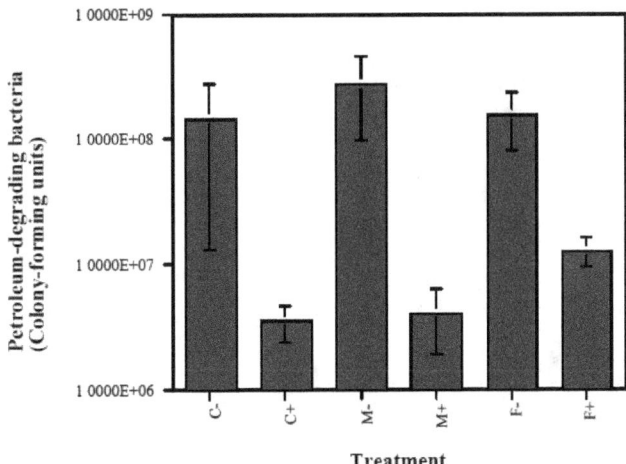

Figure 9.  Effect of bioremediation agents and oil application on petroleum-degrading bacteria 28 days after treatment.  Values are reported in colony-forming units per gram (dry weight) of soil with standard errors. C: control; M: microbial addition; F: fertilizer.  Plus signs indicate oiling and minus signs no oiling.

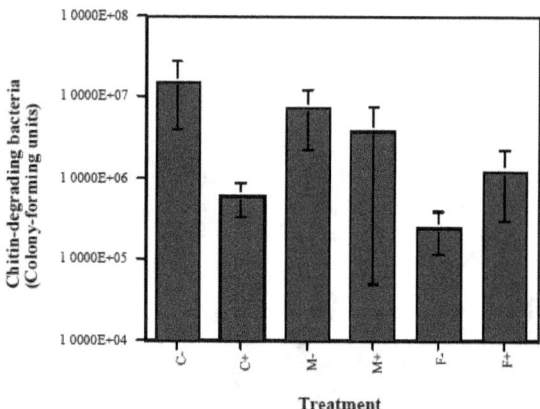

Figure 10. Effect of bioremediation agents and oil application on chitin-degrading bacteria 28 days after treatment. Values are reported in colony-forming units per gram (dry weight) of soil with standard errors. C: control; M: microbial addition; F: fertilizer. Plus signs indicate oiling and minus signs no oiling.

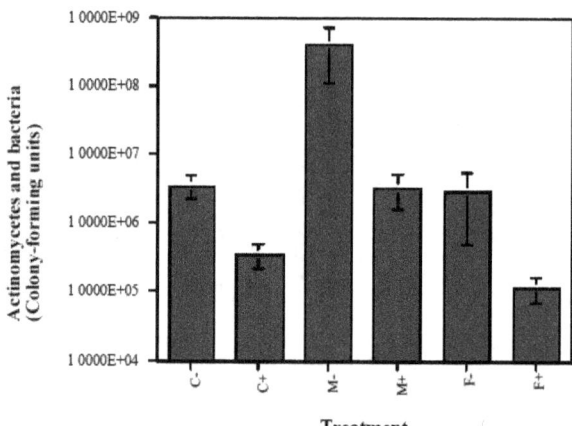

Figure 11. Effect of bioremediation agents and oil application on cellulose-degrading actinomycetes and bacteria 28 days after treatment. Values are reported in colony-forming units per gram (dry weight) of soil with standard errors. C: control; M: microbial addition; F: fertilizer. Plus signs indicate oiling and minus signs no oiling.

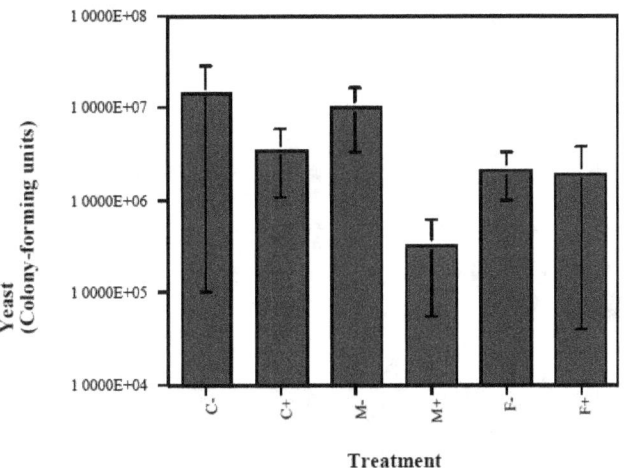

Figure 12. Effect of bioremediation agents and oil application on yeast populations 28 days after treatment. Values are reported in colony-forming units per gram (dry weight) of soil with standard errors. C: control; M: microbial addition; F: fertilizer. Plus signs indicate oiling and minus signs no oiling.

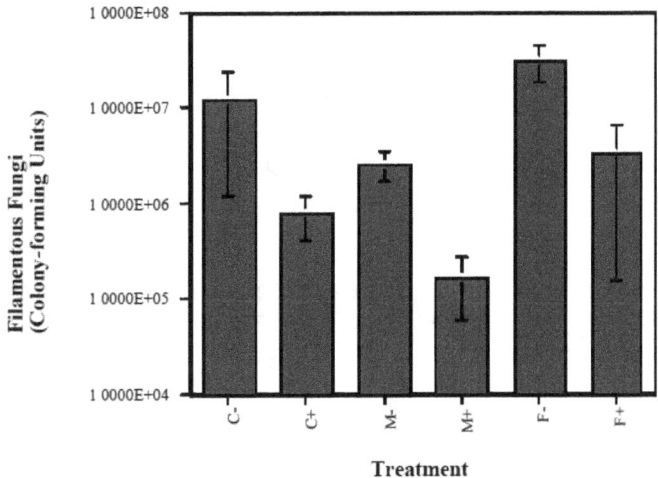

Figure 13. Effect of bioremediation agents and oil application on filamentous fungi 28 days after treatment. Values are reported in colony-forming units per gram (dry weight) of soil with standard errors. C: control; M: microbial addition; F: fertilizer. Plus signs indicate oiling and minus signs no oiling.

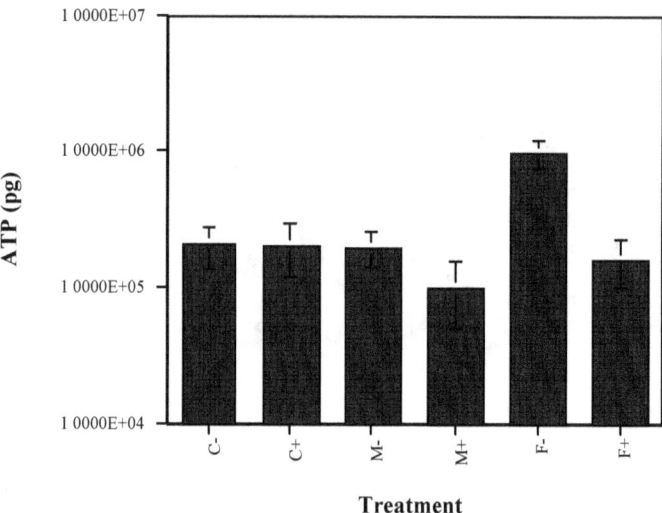

Figure 14. Effect of bioremediation agents and oil application on microbial biomass 28 days after treatment. Values are reported in picograms of ATP per gram (dry weight) of soil with standard errors. C: control; M: microbial addition; F: fertilizer. Plus signs indicate oiling and minus signs no oiling.

Table 3. Statistical Table with P-Value for Response of Microbial Populations to Bioremediation Agent and Oil Application

| Variables | Bioremediation Agent | Oil | Agent * oil |
|---|---|---|---|
| Heterotrophic | | | |
|     3 days | 0.2317 | 0.9245 | 0.8564 |
|     28 days | 0.5306 | 0.0253 | 0.4367 |
| | | | |
| Cellulose-utilizing | | | |
|     3 days | 0.1904 | 0.6170 | 0.1025 |
|     28 days | 0.1707 | 0.1770 | 0.1789 |
| | | | |
| Chitin-utilizing | | | |
|     3 days | 0.1017 | 0.4716 | 0.7436 |
|     28 days | 0.3979 | 0.1959 | 0.3269 |
| | | | |
| Yeast | | | |
|     3 days | 0.3580 | 0.3721 | 0.6048 |
|     28 days | 0.3498 | 0.1207 | 0.4486 |
| | | | |
| Fungi | | | |
|     3 days | 0.2452 | 0.2673 | 0.3263 |
|     28 days | 0.1273 | 0.0406 | 0.3034 |
| | | | |
| Petroleum-degrading | | | |
|     3 days | 0.3905 | 0.2779 | 0.5707 |
|     28 days | 0.7704 | 0.0263 | 0.7469 |
| | | | |
| ATP as biomass | | | |
|     3 days | 0.1190 | 0.3286 | 0.4179 |
|     28 days | 0.0019 | 0.0027 | 0.0022 |

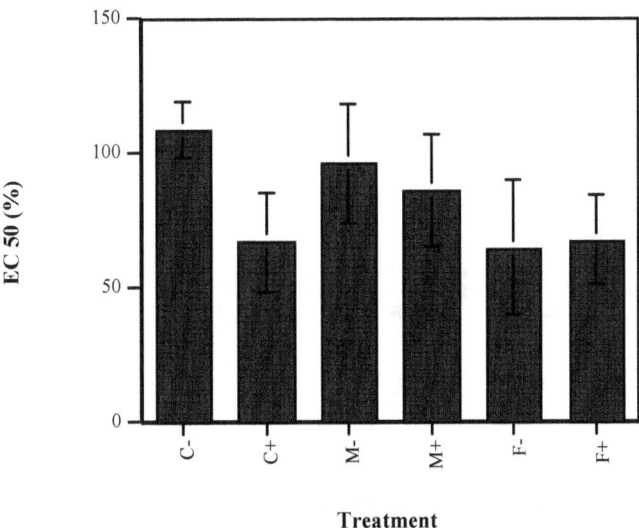

Figure 15. Effect of bioremediation agents and oil application on 15-minute readings of microtox analysis 90 days after treatment. Values are expressed as EC50 with standard errors, so higher values are less toxic than lower values. C: control; M: microbial addition; F: fertilizer. Plus signs indicate oiling and minus signs no oiling.

## Responses of Infauna to the Treatments

*Macrofauna.* The makeup of the benthic community at the beginning of the experiment and at the end of the 12 weeks was documented. The fauna was composed primarily of oligochaetes, gastropods and insects. Decapods (fiddler crabs), polychaetes, and amphipods were also represented. There were no significant differences in bioremediation agent treatments or oil levels, nor in their interactions for either number of individuals or number of species 12 weeks after the treatments. Twelve weeks after the treatments the average number of individuals was about 25/sod, and the average number of species was less than 3. The only difference was that some macrofauna populations changed with time but not due to the treatments. There was no difference in the number of individuals, but the number of species dropped significantly over the experimental period of 12 weeks. For example, the number of species decreased from 10.2 to 3.0 for the control.

Because oligochaetes often respond to organic enrichment in sediments, we tested for differences in the percentage of oligochaetes in the macrofauna community. There were no significant differences between the bioremediation agent treatments or oil levels nor in their interactions. However, by the end of the experiment, richness was significantly reduced and oligochaetes were by far the dominant fauna.

*MeiofaunA.* There were no significant differences for any of the meiofaunal groups or the copepod nematode ratio due to the bioremediation agents (Table 4). Overall, the numbers of meiofauna were usually lower in the oiled mesocosms, but the effect of oil was significant only for the number of oligochaetes and for the copepod nematode ratio. The only overall significant effect was for time (Table 4). There was a significant time effect on number of copepods, copepod nauplii and oligochaetes, but not on the number of nematodes (Table 4). There were no effects of bioremediation agent treatments or oil application on them except for those specifically mentioned (Table 4).

17

Table 4. Summary of Multiple Analysis of Variance on Four Taxa of Meiofauna and Nematode: Copepod Ratio with P-Values Provided for Main Factors and Their Interactions.

| Experiment component and interactions | Main Factors | | | Interaction | | | |
|---|---|---|---|---|---|---|---|
| | Agents | Oil | Time | Agent* Oil | Agent* time | Oil* Time | Agent* Oil* Time |
| Nematodes | 0.91 | 0.32 | 0.98 | 0.73 | 0.99 | 0.99 | 1.00 |
| Copepods | 0.18 | 0.09 | 0.0001 | 0.40 | 0.04 | 0.16 | 0.20 |
| Copepod Nauplii | 0.15 | 0.07 | 0.0001 | 0.98 | 0.02 | 0.01 | 0.10 |
| Oligochaetes | 0.06 | 0.07 | 0.0001 | 0.29 | 0.07 | 0.79 | 0.89 |
| Nematode: Copepod Ratio | 0.07 | 0.003 | 0.0001 | 0.14 | 0.15 | 0.02 | 0.30 |

Data Were Natural Log Transformed for the Analysis. Time = 1-Week, 2-Week, 4-Week and 12-Week;
Agents = Control, Fertilizer, and Microbial Seeding; Oil = Oiled and Unoiled.

Copepod Taxa

There were 11 identifiable taxa of copepods in the bioremediation samples. Some of these copepods were identified to species and family level, while some could not be identified. The most abundant groups were those associated with the *Spartina alterniflora* culms and roots (Rutledge and Fleeger 1993). Mudflat species and plankton species were rarely observed. Calanoids and other planktonic forms were not included in the data. The four most abundant copepod taxa were members of the Laophontidae, *Nannopus* spp., *Mesocra mexicana*, and *Nitocra* spp. None were affected significantly by either oil or treatment (data not shown).

*Oil Chemistry.* This study was primarily designed to evaluate toxicity of the bioremediation agents. Thus, only a limited number of samples were analyzed by detailed GC/MS for quantifying the alkane profile and specific aromatic hydrocarbons (AH)

*Normal Hydrocarbon (alkane) Profile.* Figure 16 compares the chromatographic profile of unweathered south Louisiana crude oil and laboratory weathered crude oil. Weathered oil had lost most of the lower molecular weight components through nC-13 by simple evaporation compared to the unweathered crude oil. The first normal hydrocarbon detected is nC-11 for the laboratory weathered crude oil.

Figure 17 is a chromatographic comparison of the reduced crude oil used in this experiment to the laboratory weathered crude oil. The lowest molecular weight alkane found for both oils was nC-11. The effect of vacuum distillation significantly altered the distribution pattern for the reduced crude oil, which is typical for naturally weathered crude oil. The laboratory weathered oil was altered by simple evaporation only.

Figure 18 is a chromatographic comparison of the alkane distribution for the oiled control (C+) and unoiled control (C-). Note the presence of hydrocarbons in the unoiled control. The hydrocarbon distribution is indicative of biogenic hydrocarbons, probably derived from the waxy coating covering the leaves of *Spartina alterniflora*.

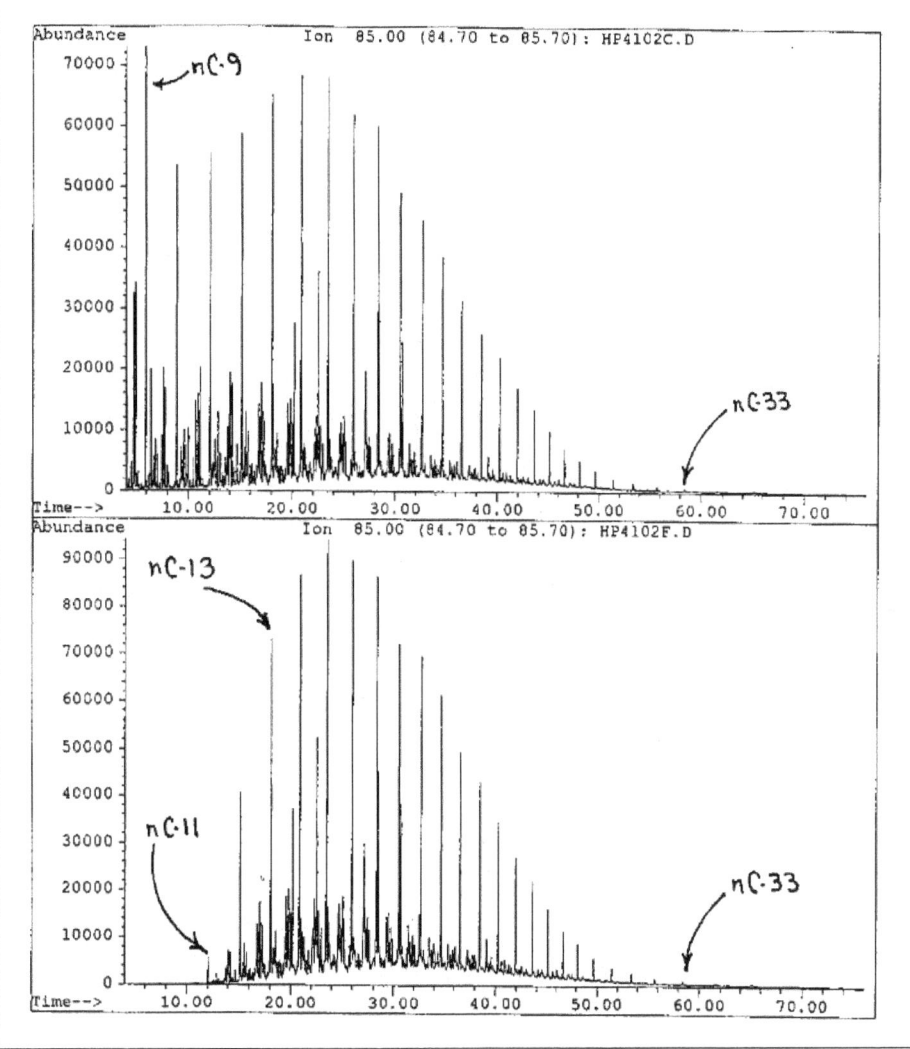

Figure 16. Chromatographic comparison of unweathered south Louisiana crude oil (top) to the laboratory weathered south Louisiana crude oil (bottom).

19

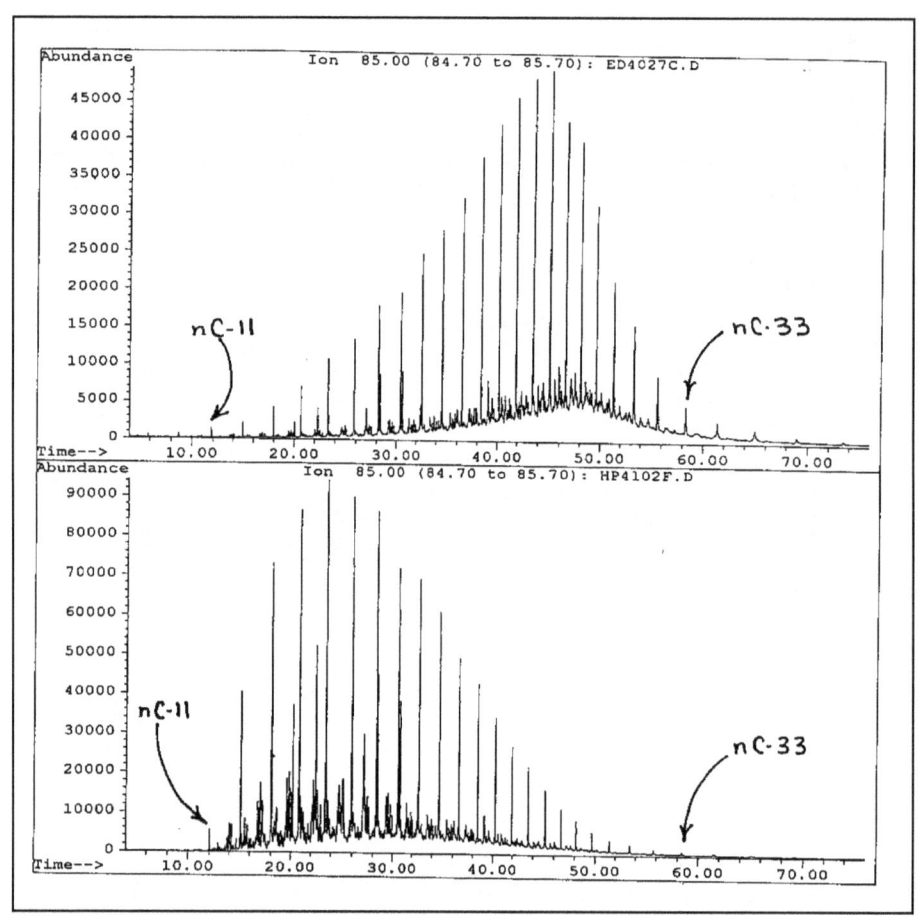

Figure 17. Chromatographic comparison of the reduced crude oil (top) used in this experiment to the laboratory weathered crude oil (bottom).

20

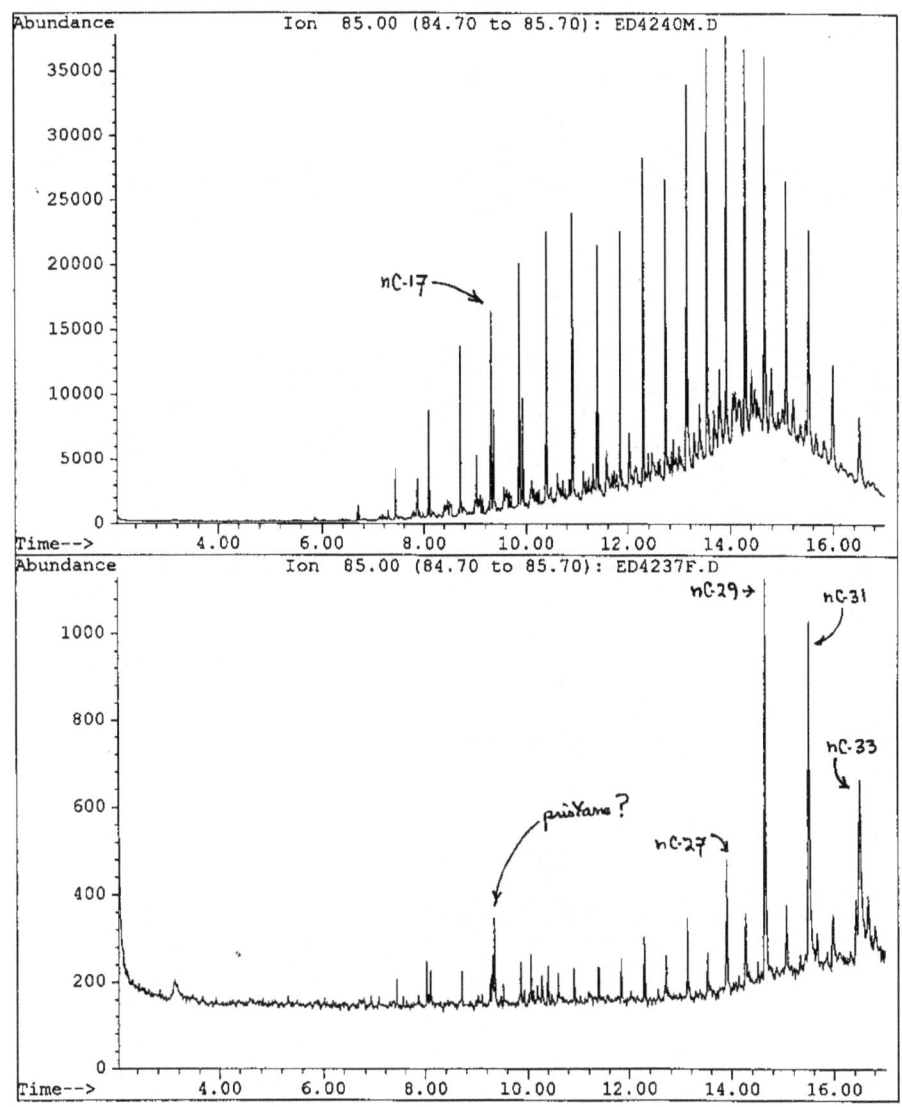

Figure 18. Chromatographic comparison of the normal hydrocarbon profile in the oiled control plot, C+ (top) compared to the unoiled control plot, C- (bottom) at Day 1.

*Composition of Selected Aromatic Hydrocarbons.* Figure 19 is a comparison of the AH profile for the reduced crude (RC) used in this experiment and the Day 1 oiled control (C+). Generally, the composition of the AH profile of RC and C+ one day after oil addition was very similar. A slight reduction in the concentration of the naphthalene and fluorene constituents is shown. The loss can probably be attributed to a combination of evaporation and dissolution between day 0 and day 1.

21

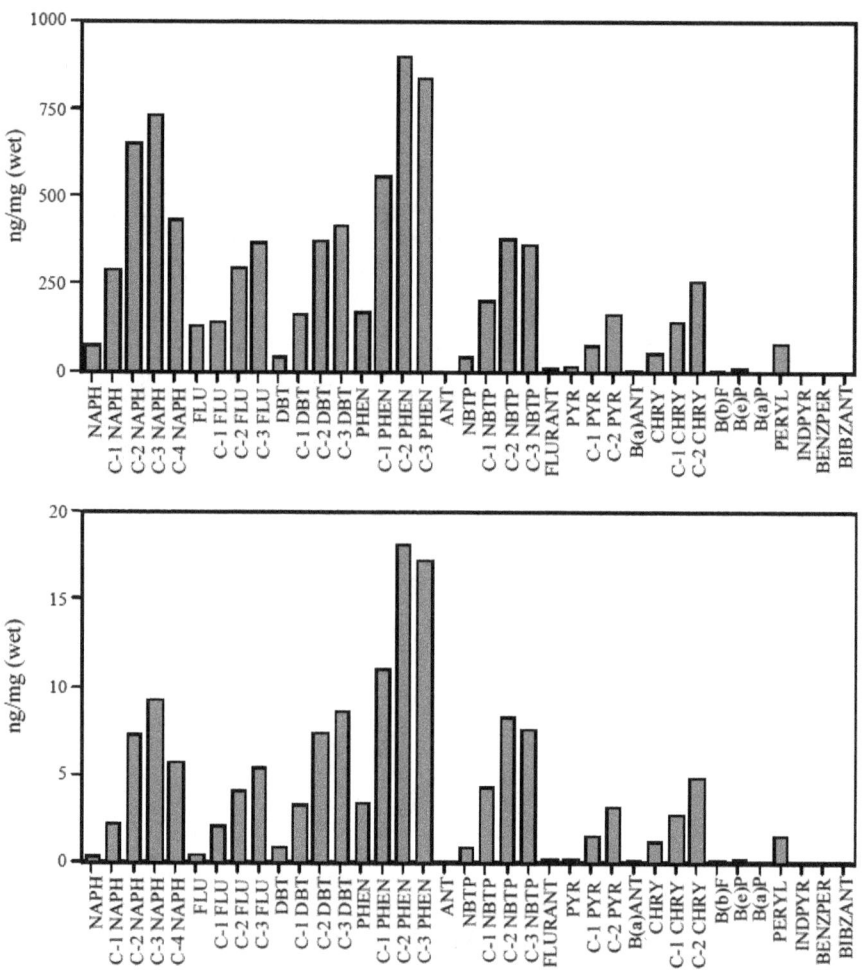

Figure 19. Aromatic hydrocarbon profile comparison between the reduced crude oil (top) and the mean C+ Day 1 values (bottom). The C+ values are derived from the mean of 3 replicate plots.

Figure 1-20 is the day 1 oiled control compared to the unoiled control for the target aromatic hydrocarbons. While the control sample does contain evidence of AH exposure, the source of the AH was combustion byproducts, not petroleum. AH derived from the incomplete combustion of fossil fuels and organic hydrocarbons are ubiquitous in the marine environment. Combustion-sourced AH is characterized by the dominance of unalkylated 3-, 4-, and 5-ring AH as opposed to petroleum-sourced AH which is dominated by 1-, 2- and 3-ring, and highly alkylated AH as exhibited in the oiled control in Figure 1-20.

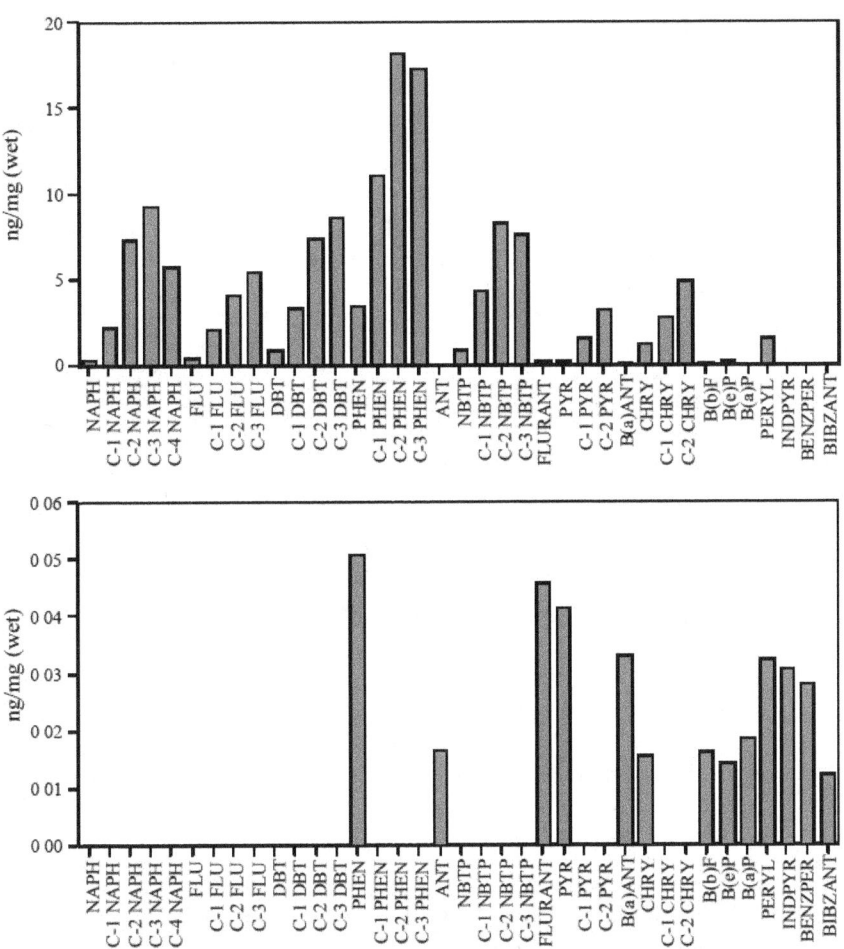

Figure 20. Aromatic hydrocarbon profile comparison between the mean C+ Day 1 values (top) and the C-, control (bottom). The C- sample is dominated by combustion derived AH while the C+ plots are dominated by the characteristic petroleum AH profile.

## Discussion

These results demonstrated that the bioremediation agents applied in this study were not toxic to the salt marsh organisms investigated. Application of bioremediation agents did not impact the macrophyte *Spartina alterniflora*, various soil microbial populations, macroinfauna, or meiofauna.

The microbial agent, Petrobac, did not adversely affect marsh plant, infaunal animals and soil microbes. Microbial seeding used in this study contains cultivated microbes and no fertilizer, and it was selected for hydrocarbon degradation in a saline medium. The marsh sods used in this study were intact natural salt marsh sections dominated by *S. alterniflora*, which contain a variety of native microbial populations naturally, including indigenous hydrocarbon-degrading microbes (Atlas 1993). When mesocosms were inoculated with Petrobac in this study, a microbial consortium that was proven to degrade petroleum in the laboratory was applied. However, the inoculated microbial populations were probably in lower abundance than the indigenous microbes in the marsh soil; thus the inoculation may not have been able to influence the microbial community composition in the sods.

Fertilizer application did not adversely affect marsh plants, infaunal animals, and microbes, but it did positively enhance the marsh plants. The Customblen (fertilizer) used in this study contained 28% N and 8% P. It is well known that nitrogen and phosphorus are essential to plants. Inorganic nutrients in salt marshes are generally not high enough for maximum plant growth. Fertilizer addition, especially nitrogen, usually enhances marsh plants (Lin and Mendelssohn 1998, 1999a; Wilsey *et al.* 1992). In fact, the fertilizer product, Customblen, stimulated plant growth, a response that was not unexpected.

The living soil community is composed of bacteria, fungi, invertebrates, and roots of *Spartina alterniflora*. The increase in soil respiration caused by the fertilizer and oil treatments could be a response to either increased microbial activity, greater root density within the soil, or both. However, the belowground live root densities of cores taken between the plants (where the respiration chamber was inserted to measure the soil respiration rate) were not significantly different among either the bioremediation agents or the oil application (data not shown). This suggests that the increased soil respiration by the application of fertilizer and oil was mainly caused by an increase in microbial activity, not by an increase in plant root respiration.

Oil application did not adversely affect the marsh plants. Oil spills may cause various acute and chronic damages, including reduced stem heights, stem density, and aboveground biomass, and increased mortality and impaired growth and regrowth (Krebs and Tanner 1981; Ferrell *et al.* 1984; Alexander & Webb 1987; Mendelssohn *et al.* 1990). In contrast, there is also evidence that oil may do little plant damage or may even stimulate growth (Burk 1977; Hershner and Moore 1977; Delaune *et al.* 1979; Li *et al.* 1990). In the present study, the absence of an adverse effect of the oil on *Spartina alterniflora* was most likely due to a low oil dosage ($1 \text{ L/m}^2$) and the relatively low toxicity of the reduced crude oil.

The typical response of benthic communities to the addition of toxic materials from chemical discharges or spills is the reduction or elimination of species or individuals (e.g., Boesch and Rabalais 1989; Rabalais *et al.* 1992). Where toxicity is not a factor, but organic enrichment of the sediments is the environmental change, a range of benthic community responses may be observed (Pearson and Rosenberg 1978). These include increases in populations of opportunistic species and reduced species diversity (e.g., Addy *et al.* 1984; Boesch and Rabalais 1989; Nance 1991). Copepod reductions during the experiment appear to be the result of mesocosm effects and elimination of potential recruitment mechanisms. Nematodes appear to be responding to organic enrichment of the sediments, from either hydrocarbons or microbial enhancement. There was no evidence of a reduced number of macro- and meio-fauna due to application of either bioremediation products. Field studies are needed to better evaluate the effect of these bioremedation products on the faunal community.

The first normal hydrocarbon detected was nC-11 for both the reduced crude oil used in this experiment and the laboratory weathered crude oil commonly used in many oil bioremediation studies. The reduced crude oil and the laboratory weathered crude oil are representative of samples collected during the first 10 days of the Greenhill Blowout near East Timbalier Island, Louisiana, for both hydrocarbon distribution pattern and degree of evaporation. Of the 22 samples collected between 3 and 13 October, 1992, the first detectable normal hydrocarbon ranged between nC-9 and nC-17 (mean nC-13, and medium nC-13). For the purpose of a bioremediation study, both reduced crude oil and laboratory weathered crude oil are acceptable since they contain a wide range of middle distillate normal hydrocarbons.

**Summary**

The bioremediation agents used in this investigation, including microbial seeding and inorganic fertilizer, had little toxicity to biota in the selected salt marsh sods. The bioremediation agents did not adversely affect the dominant marsh macrophyte, *Spartina alterniflora*, as evidenced by the plant photosynthetic rate, plant stem density, leaf elongation rate, and aboveground biomass. As expected, inorganic fertilizer application enhanced the growth of S. *alterniflora,* with significantly higher plant parameters as mentioned above. Microbial seeding had no significant effect on plant growth, and oil application also had no significant effect on plant growth. Furthermore, the bioremediation agents did not adversely affect various microbial populations, with no significant difference between the bioremediation treatments and the control for the various microbial parameters (heterotrophic microbial populations, fungi, petroleum-utilizing populations, and overall microbial biomass). In addition, the bioremediation agents did not adversely affect various infauna animals, as evidenced by no significant differences in bioremediation agent addition on either number of individuals or number of species for macrofauna and meiofauna. Overall, the bioremediation agents used at the rates in this experiment are safe to salt marsh communities, with little potential ecological impact to wetland plants, infaunal animals and microbial communities. Both reduced crude oil and laboratory weathered crude oil appear to be acceptable for bioremediation studies because they contain a wide range of middle distillate normal hydrocarbons.

# CHAPTER 2

## THE EFFECT OF BIOREMEDIATION AGENTS ON CRUDE OIL DEGRADATION AND BIOTIC RESPONSE UNDER DRAINED AND FLOODED CONDITIONS IN MARSH MESOCOSMS

by Irving A. Mendelssohn, Qianxin Lin, Karolien Debusschere, Charles B. Henry, Jr., Edward B. Overton, Ralph J. Portier, Paulene O. Roberts, and Maud M. Walsh

Many factors, especially soil physico-chemical parameters, such as oxidization status, fertility, pH, concentration of oil, and the presence of hydrocarbon degrading microbes (Alexander 1989; Blaba *et al*. 1991; Lin and Mendelssohn 1997 and 1998b; Lin et al. 1999c) may affect oil degradation. Oxygen and nutrients in wetland soils are generally not sufficient for maximum biological activity. In the application of bioremediation, the most common agents shown to enhance oil degradation are inorganic nutrients and soil aeration where, $O_2$ is deficient; microbial seeding has also been frequently used for bioremediation (Mikesell et al. 1991; Altas 1993; Bragg et al. 1993; Prince et al. 1993; Venosa et al. 1996; Lin et al. 1999c).

Previous studies (Lindstrom et al. 1991; Banks and Schwab 1993; Venosa et al. 1996; Lin and Mendelssohn 1998a and 1998b; Lin et al. 1999c) indicated that fertilization with inorganic nitrogen and phosphorus enhanced petroleum hydrocarbon degradation. Oxidants have shown to enhance oil degradation in some cases, especially for the bioremediation of petroleum-contaminated aquifers (Wang and Latchaw 1990; Lovley et al. 1994; Chapelle 1999). In addition, many microbial products have been commercialized for use in oil bioremediation, although controversial results regarding the value of microbial inocula on bioremediation have been reported (Atlas 1995a; Cassidy et al. 1997; Jorgensen et al. 2000).

Hydrology and associated inundation regimes are major-forcing functions in wetlands. Oil degradation rate can be much slower in anaerobic, water saturated soils compared to wetland soils that experience daily drainage and are less biochemically reduced (Hambrick et al. 1980; Lin and Mendelssohn 1998a). The effectiveness of bioremediation for oil spill cleanup could be greatly different under different inundation conditions. However, the effect of different inundation regimes on bioremediation has received little investigation.

The objectives of this experiment were to determine (a) the effectiveness of bioremediation with an inorganic fertilizer, a commercial microbial product, and a soil oxidant on oil degradation and (b) if inundation regime influences the effectiveness of oil bioremediation. This experiment will answer the question: Does bioremediation enhance oil degradation in intact salt marsh soil systems?

## Materials and Methods

### Experimental Design

Sixty sods of marsh (soil and vegetation intact), approximately 28 cm in diameter ($0.06$ m$^2$) and 30 cm deep, were collected from the inland zone (approximately 5 m from the creekbank natural levee) of a *Spartina alterniflora* dominated salt marsh located west of Cocodrie, Louisiana and used as the experimental units (see Chapter 1). The following treatments were randomly applied to the marsh sods: (1) microbial seeding (Petrobac), (2) fertilizer (Customblen), (3) oxidant application (Permeox) plus fertilizer (Customblen), and (4) control (no agents applied). The experimental design was a randomized block with a 4 x 2 factorial treatment arrangement (the 4 bioremediation types mentioned above) and 2 soil inundation regimes (drained and flooded conditions); all of these treatment combinations received 2 L/m$^2$ of oil and were replicated 5 times. In addition, drained and flooded controls, each replicated five times, that received neither oil nor bioremediation products were included in the experimental design so that statistical contrasts could be conducted between any of the treatment combinations within the 4 x 2 factorial design and these controls. A total of 50 sod mesocosms were used in this experiment (40 sods for the 4 x 2 factorial design and 10 additional sods for the drained and flood controls that received no oil or products).

**Experimental Procedures**

In the greenhouse, a reduced Louisiana crude with nC-13 and below removed was added to the surface water of the mesocosms at a dose of 2 L/m$^2$ (2 mm oil thickness) to the surface of 40 oiled experimental units. The other 10 experimental units received no oil or bioremediation agents and served as controls. After the applied oil was evenly spread over the surface water in the buckets, the water was drained from the bottom of the buckets to allow the oil to come in contact with and penetrate the soil of each sod.

The Customblen fertilizer used in this study contained 28% N and 8% P$_2$O$_5$ as ammonium nitrate, calcium phosphate and ammonium phosphate (Bragg et al. 1992). Petrobac contained microbial populations, without any fertilizer, selected for hydrocarbon degradation in a saline medium. PermeOx hydrolyzes when wet and converts, slowly, to Ca(OH)$_2$, CaO and H$_2$O$_2$ (hydrogen peroxide). The oxygen from the hydrogen peroxide is then catalytically released, thus, potentially accelerating aerobic microbial activity. The four bioremediation treatments (fertilizer, microbial seeding, soil oxidant plus fertilizer, and control) were applied to appropriate sods from all 40 oiled sods. The bioremediation agents were applied to the soil surface in a manner similar to that during a field application and following the manufacturer's specifications (Customblen: 93 g/m$^2$; Petrobac: 0.833 L/m$^2$ of inoculum (46 g of Petrobac/L of deionized water). In addition, 13.7 g/pot of an oxidation product (PermeOx, a product of FMC Corp., Philadelphia, PA), combined with 93 g/m$^2$ of Customblen plus 6.85 g/pot of KH$_2$PO$_4$ were applied as the oxidant treatment; KH$_2$PO$_4$ was applied to buffer the high pH that might be caused by the PermeOx according to the manufacture's instruction. Interstitial water salinity was maintained at the ambient salt marsh level (about 10 ppt). The sod-mesocosms were kept in appropriate inundation regimes: 25 sods with water table 10 cm below the soil surface, and 25 sods with 3 cm standing water over the soil surface. Water level in each experimental unit was monitored and maintained by re-watering daily.

The experiment was terminated after three months. This duration was chosen based on a review of oil spill bioremediation in saline wetland soils (Scherrer and Mille 1990; Lee and Levy 1991). During the three-month experimental period, the mesocosms were sampled for (1) petroleum hydrocarbon chemistry to identify and quantify the degree of oil biodegradation, (2) oil morphology, which was tested as an inexpensive means of evaluating oil biodegradation, (3) soil microbial response to determine the effect of the bioremediation products on the microbial communities that are performing the oil biodegradation, (4) soil chemistry to determine the effect of the bioremediation products on those factors that may limit the growth of the microbes and plants (e.g., nutrients, soil reducing conditions and soil toxins) and (5) plant response to evaluate the effects of the oil and products on plant vigor and growth.

Statistical analysis was conducted with the SAS system (SAS 1990). General Linear Model (GLM) was used to test for statistically significant differences ($P<0.05$) among the treatments and Duncan's multiple range test was used to determine significant differences among the main factors. Treatment-level combination differences, if interactions of main factors were significant, were tested with least square means.

**Methods**

Plant Response

*Photosynthetic Rate.* Leaf photosynthetic rate was measured to indicate plant growth status. A portable photosynthesis system, including an infrared gas analyzer (IRGA) (The Analytical Developmemt Co. Ltd, (ADC) model LCA-2), an ADC air flow control unit, and an ADC Parkinson leaf chamber, was used. Sample air, taken 5 m aboveground to obtain relatively stable CO$_2$ concentrations, was led through the ADC air flow control unit at the flow rate of 5 ml/s during photosynthetic rate measurements. Measurements were conducted at a quantum flux density of 2000 μmol/m$^2$/s provided by a Kodak projector lamp. An intact, attached and fully expanded young leaf was enclosed in the leaf chamber and the difference in CO$_2$ concentration and humidity between inlet and outlet air was measured. Photosynthetic rate (CO$_2$ exchange) was calculated in accordance with von Caemmerer and Farquhar (1981) and expressed as μmol CO$_2$/m$^2$/s.

*Plant Stem Density.* Plant stem density was measured by counting the number of stems in each experimental unit, expressed as the number of stems per pot.

*Average and Maximum Shoot Height.* The average shoot height and maximum shoot height of the transplants were measured to the nearest centimeter.

*Aboveground Biomass of Dominant Marsh Plants.* Plant aboveground biomass was analyzed at the end of a three-month experimental period to determine the effect of product addition on plant growth. Plant aboveground material was clipped at the soil surface. Live and dead components were separated, dried in an oven at 65°C to constant weight, and weighed.

## Soil Response

*Soil Respiration Rate.* In-situ measurements of soil respiration rate, an indicator of soil microbial activity, were made with an infra-red gas analyzer (IRGA) by measuring carbon dioxide production from soil. A PVC chamber (4 cm in diameter and 8 cm in height) with one open end was equipped with an inlet and an outlet for air flow through the chamber. The open end of the chamber was inserted into the soil 4 cm below the soil surface. An air flow rate through the chamber was held constant at 300 ml/minute by an ADC mass flow controller. The respiratory $CO_2$ produced from the soil resulted in a difference in $CO_2$ concentration between inlet and outlet that was measured by an ADC infra-red gas analyzer. Soil respiration was calculated based on the $CO_2$ exchange rate from the soil per unit surface area.

*Soil Redox Potential.* Soil redox potentials at 2 and 10 cm depths were determined with bright platinum electrodes and a calomel reference electrode. Readings were taken with a portable pH/mV digital meter. The potential of a calomel reference electrode (+244 mV) was added to each value to calculate Eh (Patrick et al. 1996).

*Soil Nutrient Concentrations.* Interstitial water samples were withdrawn from soil sods with a simple apparatus as described by McKee et al. (1988). This consisted of a small diameter (3 mm inside diameter) rigid plastic tube, containing numerous 0.5 mm diameter holes covered with 3 to 4 layers of cheesecloth, connected to a 30 ml syringe. The collected interstitial water was filtered through a 0.45 μm syringe filter. Inorganic nutrients in the filtered interstitial water were analyzed to determine the effect of product application on soil fertility and other variables. Ammonium-nitrogen ($NH_4$) and nitrate-nitrogen ($NO_3 + NO_2$) were analyzed with an auto-analyzer. Total inorganic nitrogen was determined as the sum of $NH_4$, $NO_3$, and $NO_2$-nitrogen concentrations. Phosphorus concentrations in the interstitial water were analyzed with ICP (inductively coupled argon-plasma emission spectrometer).

*Interstitial pH and Salinity.* Interstitial water samples were withdrawn from soil as previously described. Interstitial pH was measured with a digital pH meter and interstitial salinity was measured with a salt refractometer.

## Microbial Response

Determining the response of the salt marsh microbial component of the ecosystem was accomplished by measuring general microbial heterotrophic populations, cellulose-utilizing populations, chitin-utilizing populations, yeast and fungi, petroleum-utilizing populations, and overall microbial biomass. Samples were collected at the end of the experiment for the Microtox toxicity assay.

Samples of marsh soil were collected with a 5 cc syringe with the end cut off and the remaining edge sharpened to facilitate penetration into the soil. Samples for microbial analysis were taken from the top 3 cm in two locations in the pot for each sampling episode. The two samples were mixed to form a composite sample. General microbial populations and oil-degrading were tracked using plate count methods on a variety of selective agars. Nutrient agar (Difco) was used to grow general heterotrophic populations. A minimal salts agar to which 50 ppm naphthalene and 50 ppm cresol were added as the sole carbon source was used for the selective culturing of petroleum-degrading organisms. General microbial biomass was measured using the adenosine triphosphate method (Bianchini et al. 1988). All microbial population measurements were reported per gram dry weight gram.

<u>Residual Oil Chemistry in the Soil.</u>

The top 5 cm of soil from each sod was collected with the same technique as for the microbial samples, thoroughly homogenized, and extracted using a modified EPA method 3550. Approximately 20 grams of wet sediment were extracted using dichloromethane and sodium sulfate as a chemical drying agent (Venosa et al. 1996; Sauer and Boehm 1991; Henry and Overton 1993; Henry et al. 1993), then reduced to a final volume of 10 ml. A field treatment composite was then analyzed by gas chromatography-mass spectrometry (GC/MS) operated in the Selective Ion Monitoring (SIM) Mode to characterize compositional changes in targeted normal hydrocarbons (NH) and aromatic hydrocarbons (AH). Although these targeted AH generally represent less than 5% of the bulk oil composition, they are essential to characterize petroleum sources, identify potential biological effects, determine exposure pathways, and monitor weathering trends and degradation of the oil (Sauer and Boehm 1991; Roques et al. 1994). The targeted aromatic hydrocarbons are listed in Table 1 in Chapter 1.

In addition, oil morphology was documented in this experiment. The detailed methods of oil morphology are attached in Appendix B.

**Results**

<u>Responses of *S. alterniflora* to the Treatments</u>

The effect of the bioremediation agents and oil on *Spartina alterniflora* were estimated by measuring leaf elongation rate, photosynthetic rate, relative growth rates based on stem density and cumulative shoot height, and aboveground biomass. Similar to our observations in the toxicity experiment in Chapter 1, the fertilizer had a significant positive effect on leaf elongation (Fig. 21), photosynthetic rate (Fig. 22), relative growth rates (Figs. 23A and 23B), and live aboveground biomass (Fig. 24) (Table 5). However, the addition of the oxidant (PermeOx) somewhat counteracted the enhancing effect of the fertilizer on live aboveground biomass (Fig. 24) although the treatment of the soil oxidant plus fertilizer still significantly increased plant growth responses compared with the control. In addition, microbial seeding had no significant effect on plant growth responses (Figs. 21 to 24) compared to the controls. The addition of oil did not significantly affect plant growth responses (Figs. 21 to 24). The inundation treatment also had no significant effect on plant growth responses (Table 5).

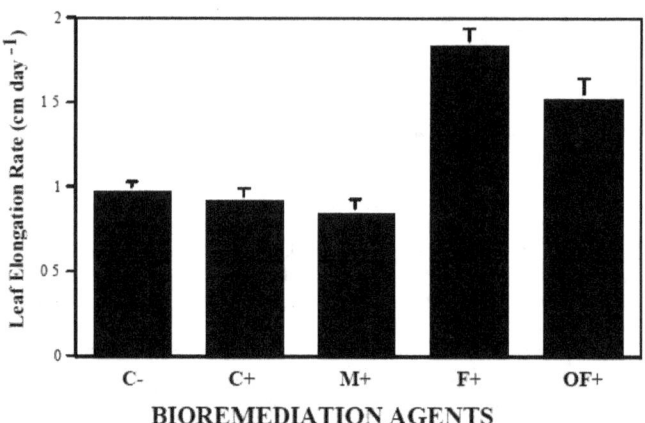

Figure 21. Effect of bioremediation agents on leaf elongation of *Spartina alterniflora*. Values are means averaged over inundation treatments and times of 4, 8, and 12 weeks after the bioremediation treatment (n=30). Standard errors are presented. C=control; M=microbial seeding; F=fertilizer; OF=oxidant plus fertilizer. Plus signs indicate oiling, and minus signs no oiling.

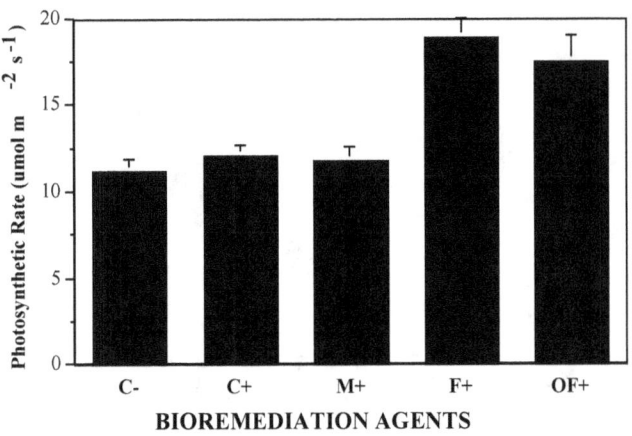

Figure 22. Effect of bioremediation agents on photosynthetic rate of *Spartina alterniflora*. Values are means averaged over inundation treatments and times of 4 and 12 weeks after the bioremediation treatment (n=20). Standard errors are presented. C=control; M=microbial seeding; F=fertilizer; OF= oxidant plus fertilizer. Plus signs indicate oiling, and minus signs no oiling.

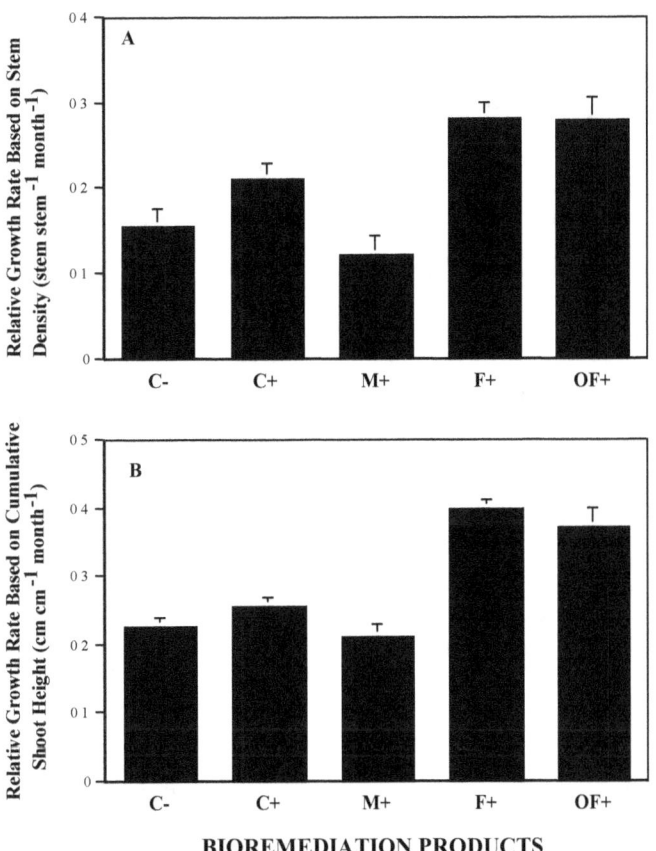

Figure 23. Effect of bioremediation agents on stem growth rate (A) and cumulative shoot growth rate (B) of *Spartina alterniflora*. Values are means averaged over inundation treatments (n=10). Standard errors are presented. C=control; M=microbial seeding; F=fertilizer; OF= oxidant plus fertilizer. Plus signs indicate oiling, and minus signs no oiling.

31

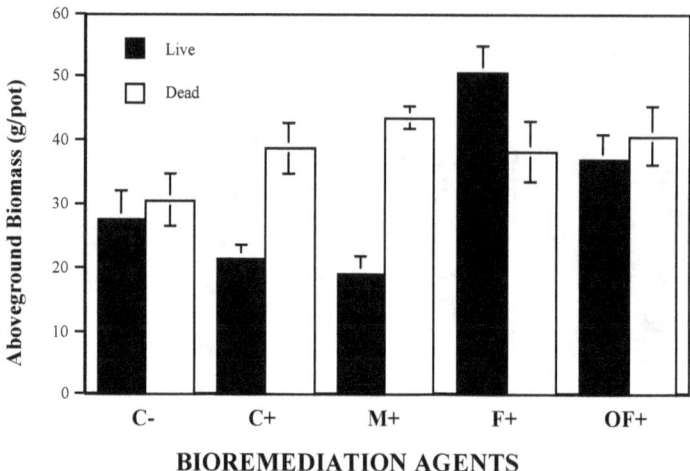

Figure 24. Effect of bioremediation agents on aboveground biomass of *Spartina alterniflora*. Values are means averaged over inundation treatments (n=10). Standard errors are presented. C=control; M=microbial seeding; F=fertilizer; OF= oxidant plus fertilizer. Plus signs indicate oiling, and minus signs no oiling.

Table 5. Statistical Table for Plant and Soil Variables with P-Values Provided for Main Factors and Their Interactions.

| Parameter | Main Factors | | | Interaction | | | |
|---|---|---|---|---|---|---|---|
| | Agents | Inund | Time | Agents* Inund | Agent* Time | Inundation* Time | Agent* Inundation* Time |
| Leaf Elongation (4, 8, 12-wks) | 0.0001 | 0.8699 | 0.0001 | 0.2333 | 0.0787 | 0.3158 | 0.5933 |
| RGR Stem 0-12 wk | 0.0003 | 0.4742 | | 0.7068 | | | |
| RGR of Height 0-12 | 0.0001 | 0.8684 | | 0.9067 | | | |
| Photosynthetic rate (4 and 12 wk) | 0.0001 | 0.8823 | 0.0001 | 0.9296 | 0.6851 | 0.9408 | 0.1674 |
| Live Aboveground Biomass | 0.0001 | 0.3566 | | 0.1389 | | | |
| Dead Aboveground Biomass | 0.7825 | 0.5720 | | 0.3986 | | | |
| Total Aboveground Biomass | 0.0001 | 0.3566 | | 0.1389 | | | |
| Resp (2,4,8,12) | 0.0001 | 0.0001 | 0.0672 | 0.0001 | 0.0107 | 0.0001 | 0.0006 |
| Eh at 2 cm (1,2,4,12 wks) | 0.2595 | 0.0001 | 0.0598 | 0.3346 | 0.5154 | 0.0060 | 0.4725 |
| Eh at 12 cm 1,2,4,12 wks) | 0.8033 | 0.0004 | 0.0001 | 0.8828 | 0.1547 | 0.0499 | 0.1997 |

Agents: Bioremediation Agents; Inund: Inundation regimes; Time: Sampling Time; Agent*Inund: Bioremediation Agents by Inundation Regime Interaction

Soil parameters such as Eh, interstitial sulfide, salinity, pH and nutrients were measured to determine if the bioremediation products, oil, and inundation regimes had any effect on soil condition. The addition of the products and oil did not significantly affect soil redox potential (Eh) at 2 and 12 cm depths. However, as expected, Eh was significantly higher in the drained inundation regime compared with the flood regime (Figs. 25A and B) (Table 5). The application of the bioremediation agents and oil did not significantly affect interstitial salinity (data not shown). Generally, the products and oil, and the inundation regimes did not significantly affect interstitial pH (Fig 26).

Fertilization, as expected, increased interstitial inorganic nitrogen (ammonia plus nitrate) concentration throughout the three-month experimental period, with significantly higher nitrogen concentration in the fertilizer and oxidant plus fertilizer treatments (Fig. 27A) compared to the control and microbial seeding treatments. Microbial seeding did not significantly affect interstitial inorganic nitrogen concentration compared to the control. The interstitial phosphorus concentrations in the oxidant treatment were significantly higher than those of the other treatments most likely due to the use of $KH_2PO_4$ in the oxidant treatment to buffer a possible pH increase by PermeOx (Fig. 27B). However, the fertilizer and microbial treatments did not affect interstitial phosphorus concentrations compared to the control.

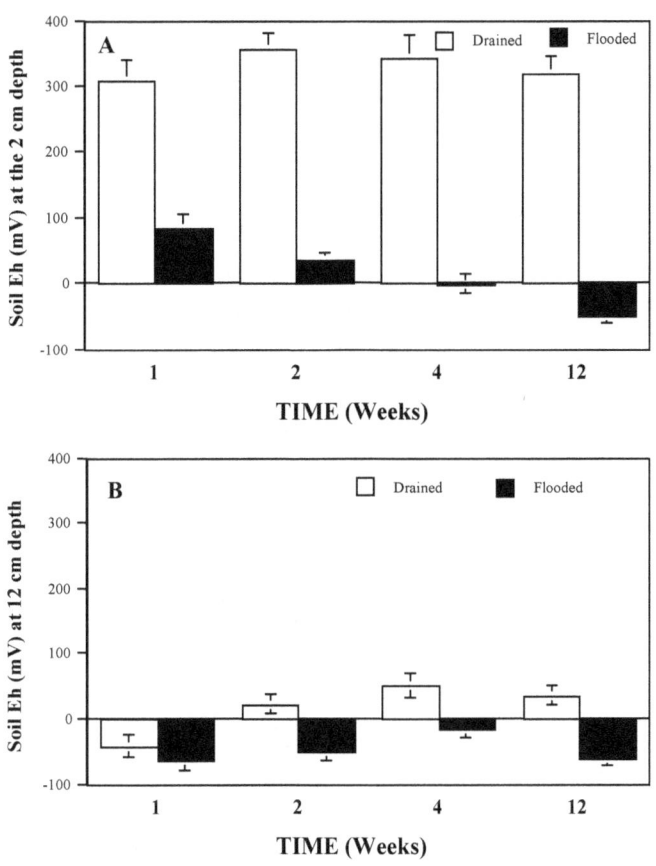

Figure 25. Effect of inundation regime on soil redox potential at the depth of 2 cm (A) and 12 cm (B) below the soil surface. Values are means averaged over bioremediation agents and oil application (n=25). Standard errors are presented.

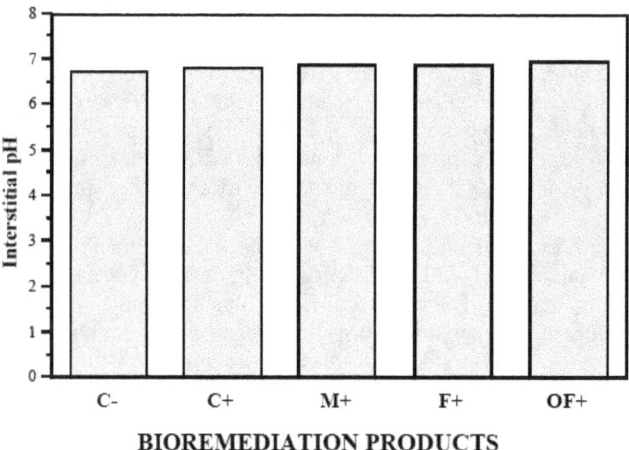

Figure 26. Effect of bioremediation agents on interstitial pH of *Spartina alterniflora*. Values are means averaged over inundation treatments and time of 2, 4, 8, and 12 weeks after the treatment (n=40). C=control; M=microbial seeding; F=fertilizer; OF= oxidant plus fertilizer. Plus signs indicate oiling, and minus signs no oiling. Note: Standard errors are small, and bars not apparent.

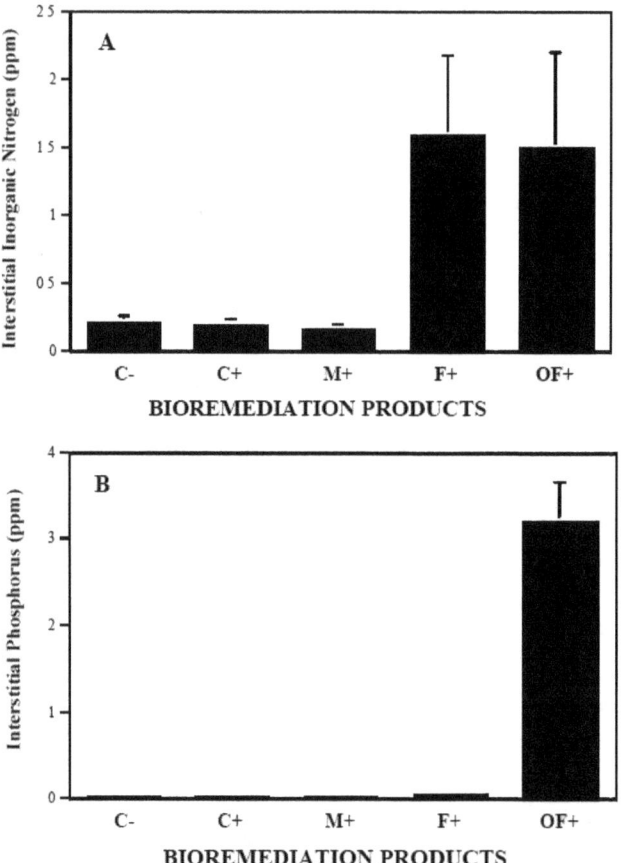

Figure 27. Effect of bioremediation agents on interstitial inorganic nitrogen (A) and phosphorus (B). Values are means averaged over inundation treatments and time of 1, 2, 4, and 12 weeks after the treatment (n=40). Standard errors are presented. C=control; M=microbial seeding; F=fertilizer; OF= oxidant plus fertilizer. Plus signs indicate oiling, and minus signs no oiling.

## Responses of Microbes to the Treatments

Soil respiration was measured at 2, 4, 8 and 12 weeks after the treatments to determine the effects of the bioremediation products, oil, and inundation regimes on the metabolism of the soil community (Fig. 28). Generally, soil respiration rates in the drained regime were significantly higher than those in the flooded regime (Figs. 28 A, B, C and D) (Table 5). Surprisingly, the addition of the oxidant plus fertilizer to oiled pots in the drained regime (OF+L) sharply increased soil respiration. Soil respiration of the OF+L treatment was significantly ($p < 0.0001$) higher than that of the other treatments 2, 4 and 8 weeks after bioremediation with the peak soil respiration at week 2 and 4 (Figs. 28 A, B, and C). This dramatic increase in soil respiration was most likely due to an increase in soil microbial activity. In addition, fertilizer significantly increased soil respiration 12 weeks after the bioremediation treatment (Fig. 28 D).

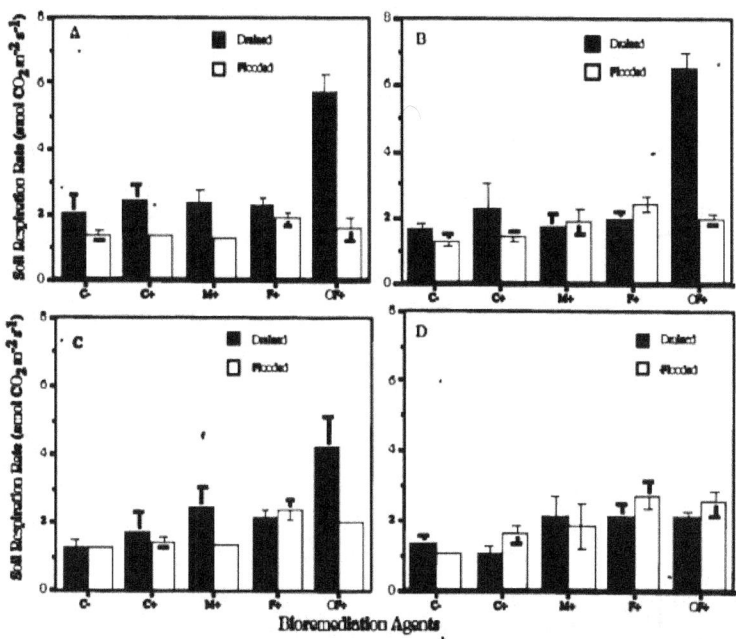

Figure 28. Effect of bioremediation agents on soil respiration rate 2 (A), 4 (B), 8 (C), and 12 (D) weeks after the bioremediation treatment. Values are means (n=5) with standard errors. C=control; M=microbial seeding; F=fertilizer; OF=oxidant plus fertilizer. Plus signs indicate oiling, and minus signs no oiling.

Bioremediation stimulated soil heterotrophic bacteria, especially in the oxidant plus fertilizer treatment. Even at the start of the experiment, treatment effects were noted in some cases; a sampling was several hours after the treatment application and because bacteria generally have a doubling time on the order of minutes or hours, bacterial responses to the treatments occurred early in the experiment. Soil oxidant plus fertilizer addition showed statistically higher populations of heterotrophic bacteria than all other treatments (Fig. 29) in both flooded and drained inundation regimes, but no significant difference in petroleum-degrading bacteria (Fig. 30).

At week 3, both heterotrophic (Fig. 31) and petroleum-degrading bacteria (Fig. 32) had significantly higher population counts in the flooded, oxidizer plus fertilizer treatment than for any other treatment. Under drained conditions, week 3 showed significantly higher petroleum-degrading populations in mesocosms treated with oxidizer and fertilizer. Neither ATP values (Fig. 35) nor heterotrophic populations showed significant differences among bioremediation treatments for the drained treatment.

At week 12, heterotrophic bacteria in the flooded and drained treatment again showed significantly higher numbers for the oxidant and fertilizer combination than in the other treatments (Fig. 33). There were higher numbers of petroleum-degrading bacteria for the oxidant plus fertilizer treatment in the flooded regime compared to the other treatments (Fig. 34). ATP values showed no significant differences (Fig. 36).

35

**Oil Morphology**

<u>Efficacy of the Bioremediation Products</u>

The presence or absence and extent of different oil morphologies indicative of biodegradation in the various application series were used to compare relative degrees of degradation between the various product-applications throughout the experiment. The results of this evaluation are presented in Tables 5 and 6 and summarized below.

Oil morphological observations indicated that six days after product-application, the oxidant plus fertilizer marsh sods started to exhibit oil characteristics that were indicative of biodegradation (paste). By the eighth day, oil in the drained oxidant plus fertilizer treatment showed an enhancement of biodegradation (organic coat) as compared to the other product-applications and flooding regimes. The only other marsh sods in which oil morphologies indicative of biodegradation were observed were the drained fertilized treatments.

While other treatments also were characterized by some degradation at this time, the process was not as advanced as in the oxidant plus fertilizer treatment or even the fertilizer treatment. In the control and microbial seeding treatments, no obvious differences in oil morphologies could be recognized to determine relative degrees of biodegradation between the two flooding regimes. Oil was generally moist and creamy during these first observations and oil degradation was generally most advanced in the oxidant plus fertilizer followed by the fertilizer, control, and microbial treatments (Tables 6 and 7).

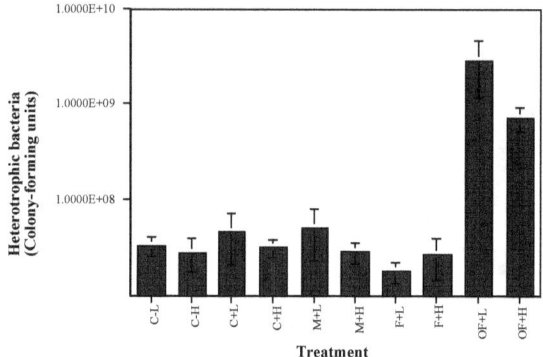

Figure 29. Effect of bioremediation agents on heterotrophic bacteria 6 hours after the bioremediation treatment. Values are means in colony-forming units per gram (dry weight) of soil (n=5) with standard errors. C=control; M=microbial seeding; F=fertilizer; OF= oxidant plus fertilizer. Plus signs indicate oiling, and minus signs no oiling. H indicates flooded mesocosms and L Drained.

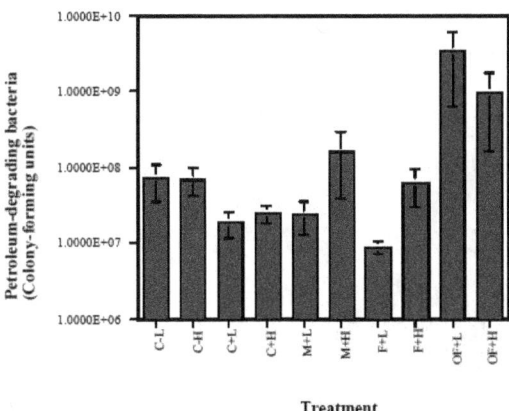

Figure 30. Effect of bioremediation agents on petroleum-degrading bacteria 6 hours after the bioremediation treatment. Values are means in colony-forming units per gram (dry weight) of soil (n=5) with standard errors. C=control; M=microbial seeding; F=fertilizer; OF= oxidant plus fertilizer. Plus signs indicate oiling, and minus signs no oiling. H indicates flooded mesocosms and L Drained.

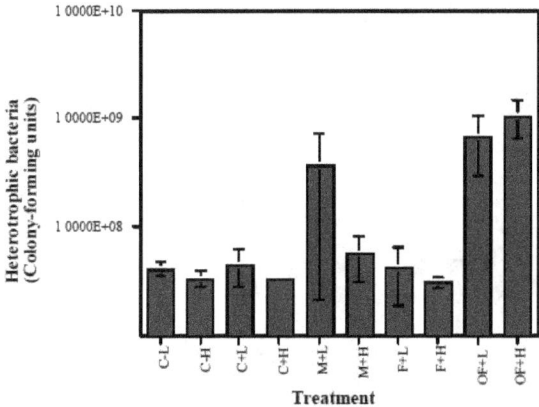

Figure 31. Effect of bioremediation agents on heterotrophic bacteria 3 weeks after the bioremediation treatment. Values are means in colony-forming units per gram (dry weight) of soil (n=5) with standard errors. C=control; M=microbial seeding; F=fertilizer; OF= oxidant plus fertilizer. Plus signs indicate oiling, and minus signs no oiling. H indicates flooded mesocosms and L Drained.

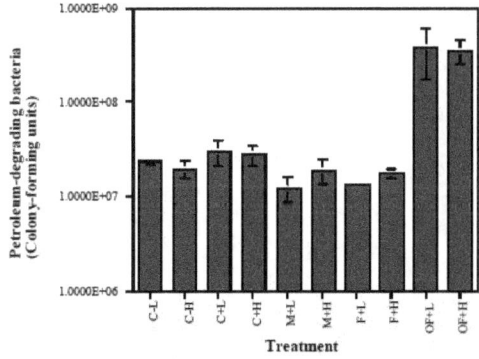

Figure 32. Effect of bioremediation agents on petroleum-degrading bacteria 3 weeks after the bioremediation treatment. Values are means in colony-forming units per gram (dry weight) of soil (n=5) with standard errors. C=control; M=microbial seeding; F=fertilizer; OF= oxidant plus fertilizer. Plus signs indicate oiling, and minus signs no oiling. H indicates flooded mesocosms and L Drained.

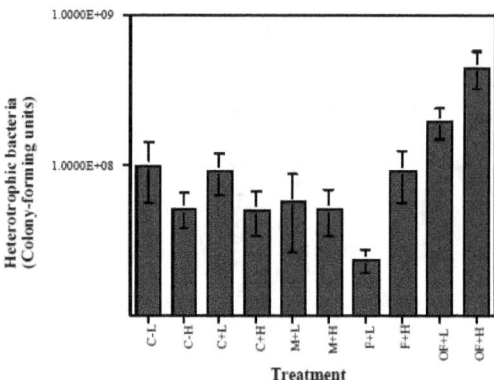

Figure 33. Effect of bioremediation agents on heterotrophic bacteria 12 weeks after the bioremediation treatment. Values are means in colony-forming units per gram (dry weight) of soil (n=5) with standard errors. C=control; M=microbial seeding; F=fertilizer; OF= oxidant plus fertilizer. Plus signs indicate oiling, and minus signs no oiling. H indicates flooded mesocosms and L Drained.

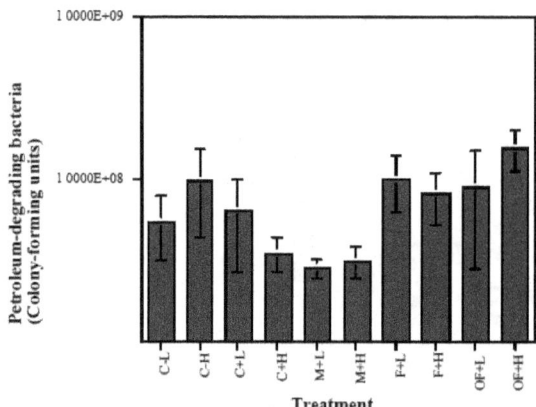

Figure 34. Effect of bioremediation agents on petroleum-degrading bacteria 12 weeks after the bioremediation treatment. Values are means in colony-forming units per gram (dry weight) of soil (n=5) with standard errors. C=control; M=microbial seeding; F=fertilizer; OF= oxidant plus fertilizer. Plus signs indicate oiling, and minus signs no oiling. H indicates flooded mesocosms and L Drained.

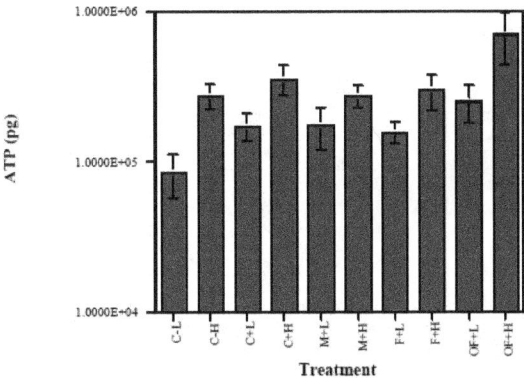

Figure 35. Effect of bioremediation agents on microbial biomass 3 weeks after the bioremediation treatment. Values are means in picograms of ATP per gram (dry weight) of soil (n=5) with standard errors. C=control; M=microbial seeding; F=fertilizer; OF= oxidant plus fertilizer. Plus signs indicate oiling, and minus signs no oiling. H indicates flooded mesocosms and L Drained.

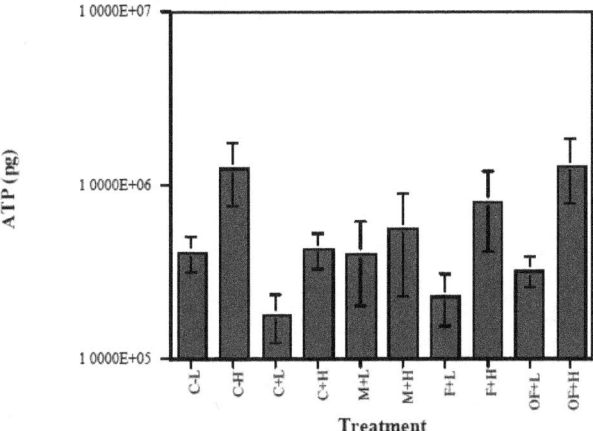

Figure 36. Effect of bioremediation agents on microbial biomass 12 weeks after the bioremediation treatment. Values are means in picograms of ATP per gram (dry weight) of soil (n=5) with standard errors. C=control; M=microbial seeding; F=fertilizer; OF= oxidant plus fertilizer. Plus signs indicate oiling, and minus signs no oiling. H indicates flooded mesocosms and L Drained.

Table 6.  Relative Degree of Degradation for Each of the Observations
by Inundation Regime and Product Application (*) Estimated by Oil Morphology.

| | Day 2 | | Day 6 | | Day 8 | | Day 21 | | Day 35 | | Day 49 | | Day 93 | |
|---|---|---|---|---|---|---|---|---|---|---|---|---|---|---|
| | L | H | L | H | L | H | L | H | L | H | L | H | L | H |
| C+ | 1 | 4 | 3 | 3 | 3 | 3/2 | 3/4 | 3 | 3 | 3 | 4 | 3 | 3 | 4 |
| F+ | 1 | 2 | 2 | 2 | 2 | 2/3 | 2 | 1/2 | 1/2 | 1 | 2/3 | 2/1 | 4 | 2 |
| M+ | 1 | 3 | 2 | 2 | 4 | 4 | 4/3 | 4 | 4 | 4 | 1 | 4 | 2 | 1 |
| OF+ | 1 | 1 | 1 | 1 | 1 | 1 | 1 | 2/1 | 2/1 | 2 | 3/2 | 1/2 | 1 | 3 |

Product applications are ranked on a scale of 1 to 4 on relative degradation effectiveness (1=highest, 4=lowest).

Table 7.  Relative Degree of Degradation for Each of the Observations Periods
and Total Score of Degradation-Effectiveness by Product-Application (**).

| | Day 2 | Day 6 | Day 8 | Day 21 | Day 35 | Day 49 | Day 93 | TOTAL |
|---|---|---|---|---|---|---|---|---|
| C | 5 | 6 | 5.5 | 6.5 | 6 | 7 | 7 | **43.0** |
| F | 4 | 4 | 4.5 | 3.5 | 2.5 | 4 | 6 | **28.5** |
| M | 4 | 4 | 8 | 7.5 | 8 | 5 | 3 | **39.5** |
| OF | 2 | 2 | 2 | 2.5 | 3.5 | 4 | 4 | **20.0** |

A small number in total indicates a high degradation effectiveness.
(*)     If differences between applications were observed to be minimal, the score consisted of a range with the first
        score being the dominant rating (e.g., 2/1 or 1/2).  If no differences were noted, applications were given the
        same score.
(**)    Scores are derived by adding individual scores for the L and H inundation regimes from Table 2-1 for each
        observation.  These composite scores were subsequently added to provide the total score for each
        bioremediation product.
        C     = Control
        F     = Fertilizer
        M     = Microbial seeding
        OF    = Oxidant and fertilizer
        L     = Drained Regime
        H     = Flood Regime

        The overall effectiveness to enhance biodegradation for each of the treatments is presented in the last
column of Table 7.  This overall-score was derived by adding the individual scores for the each of the observations
by product-application.  The results indicate that the oxidant plus fertilizer was the most effective of all
bioremediation products in enhancing biodegradation throughout the 12 week period while the microbial seeding
was the least effective.

Oil Chemistry

*Alkane Degradation.* The nC-18/phytane ratio was used, in part, to evaluate normal alkane degradation. Bioremediation enhanced alkane degradation. Both the fertilizer and the soil oxidant plus fertilizer treatments significantly increased alkane degradation, with significantly lower nC-18/phytane in these treatments compared to the controls 3 and 5 weeks after the treatment (Fig. 37) (Table 8). Furthermore, alkane degradation was significantly higher in the drained treatment than in the flooded treatment three and five weeks after the treatment. However, microbial seeding application did not significantly affect alkane degradation. All of the treatments including the controls reduced the resolvable alkane profile such that few resolvable alkanes remained, predominately isoprenoids. Since the alkane constituents are so easily degraded, even without bioremediation, they should not be a primary parameter to assess efficacy.

*Aromatic Hydrocarbon Degradation.* The effect of bioremediation on aromatic hydrocarbon degradation appeared to increase with the time after the treatment. Three weeks after treatment application, neither bioremediation agents nor inundation treatment had a significant effect on aromatic hydrocarbon degradation (Fig. 38). However, five weeks after application, TTAH concentration in the treatment receiving soil oxidant plus fertilizer under the drained condition was significantly lower than the other treatments (Fig. 38). However, the other bioremediation agents had no significant effect on TTAH concentration compared to the control. TTAH concentration was significantly lower in the drained treatment than in the flooded treatment 5 weeks after the bioremediation application. Twelve weeks after the bioremediation application, TTAH concentrations in the treatments receiving fertilizer and treatments receiving oxidant plus fertilizer were significantly lower than the control (Fig. 38) (Table 8).

Variance usually can be reduced by normalizing the data to degradative-resistant compounds contained within the oil itself. One technique is the use of hopane as an internal standard. The ratio of TTAH/hopane was significantly lower in the treatment receiving the soil oxidant plus fertilizer under the drained condition compared to the control 5 and 12 weeks after the treatment (Fig. 39) (Table 8). The ratio of TTAH/hopane was significantly lower in the treatment receiving fertilizer compared to the control 3 and 5 weeks after the treatment, but not for 12 weeks after the treatment. Microbial seeding did not significantly affect the ratio of TTAH/hopane. A large variability in the hydrocarbon data due to a patchy oil distribution resulting from an uneven soil surface made it difficult to detect treatment differences.

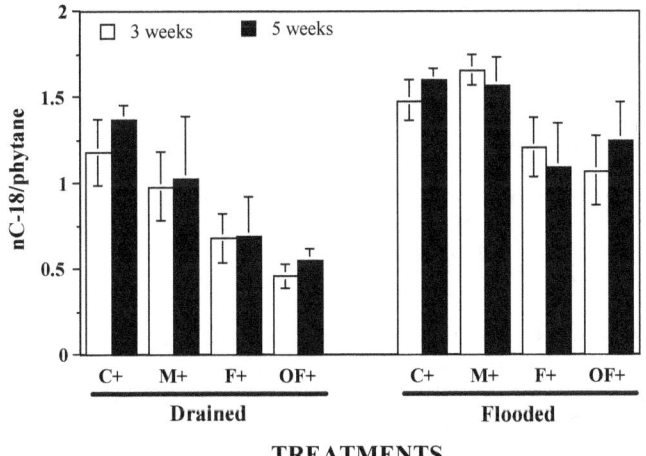

Figure 37. Effect of bioremediation agents on alkane degradation 3 and 5 weeks after the bioremediation treatment. Values are means (n=5) with standard errors. C=control; M=microbial seeding; F=fertilizer; OF= oxidant plus fertilizer. Plus signs indicate 2 l m$^{-2}$ of oil addition at the beginning of the experiment.

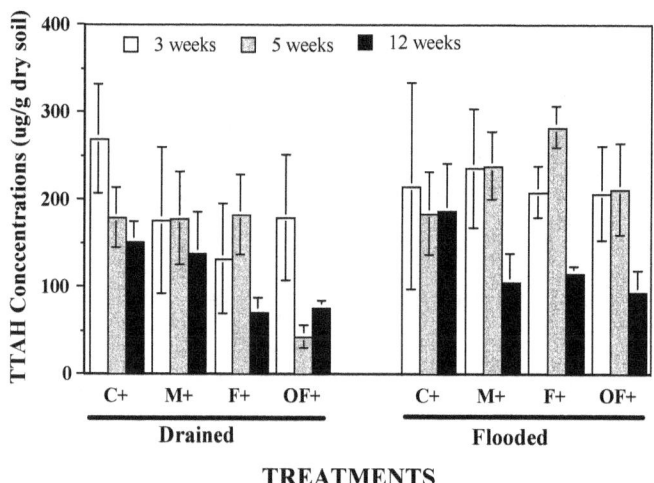

Figure 38. Effect of bioremediation agents on the residual total targeted aromatic hydrocarbon concentrations 3, 5, and 12 weeks after the bioremediation treatment. Values are means (n=5) with standard errors. C=control; M=microbial seeding; F=fertilizer; OF=oxidant plus fertilizer. Plus signs indicate 2 L/m$^2$ of oil addition at the beginning of the experiment.

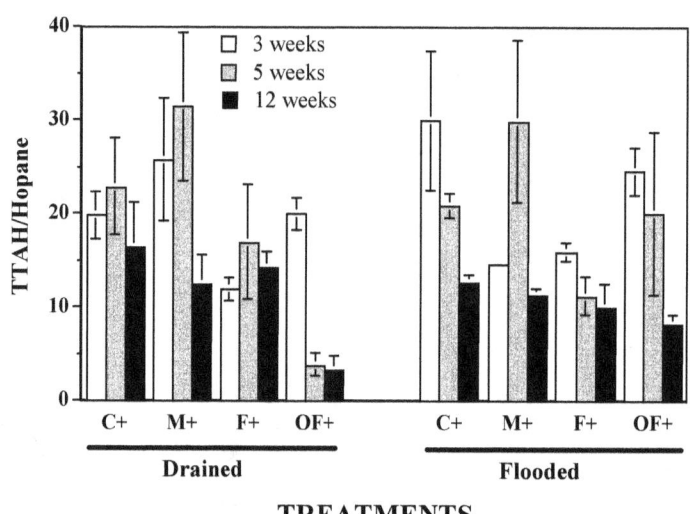

Figure 39. Effect of bioremediation agents on the residual total targeted aromatic hydrocarbon normalized to hopane 3, 5, and 12 weeks after the bioremediation treatment. Values are means (n=5) with standard errors. C=control; M=microbial seeding; F=fertilizer; OF=oxidant plus fertilizer. Plus signs indicate 2 L/m$^2$ of oil addition at the beginning of the experiment.

Table 8. Statistical Table for the Oil Chemistry Variables
with P-Values Provided for Main Factors and Their Interactions

| Parameter | Agents | Inund | Agent*Inund |
|---|---|---|---|
| n-C18/phytane (3 week) | 00021 | 0.0001 | 0.0001 |
| n-C18/phytane (5 week) | 0.0305 | 0.0067 | 0.7947 |
| TTAH (3 week) | 0.7966 | 0.6023 | 0.8166 |
| TTAH (5 week) | 0.0955 | 0.0123 | 0.3095 |
| TTAH (12 week) | 0.0874 | 0.4138 | 0.8799 |
| TTAH/Hopane (3 week) | 0.0356 | 0.4750 | 0.0401 |
| TTAH/Hopane (5 week) | 0.0300 | 0.7025 | 0.3003 |
| TTAH/Hopane (12 week) | 0.0067 | 0.5295 | 0.2073 |

Agents: Bioremediation Agents; Inund: Inundation Regimes; Time: Sampling Time; Agent*Inund: Bioremediation Agents by Inundation Regime Interaction

## Discussion

In the present study, fertilizer application significantly enhanced plant growth in the treatments receiving fertilizer and the soil oxidant plus fertilizer, but microbial seeding application had no effect. Soil oxidant application combined with fertilization and the pH buffer, $KH_2PO_4$, significantly enhanced soil parameters such as soil interstitial phosphorus concentration, soil respiration rate, and soil microbial counts. More importantly, concentrations of residual aromatic hydrocarbons were significantly lower in the treatment receiving soil oxidant plus fertilizer compared to the control. Generally, microbial seeding did not affect oil degradation compared to the control.

We used a slow-release fertilizer containing 28% N, 8% $P_2O_5$ (or 3% P), and 0% K in the present experiment. As a result, fertilizer application significantly increased interstitial nitrogen concentration in the treatments receiving fertilizer and soil oxidant plus fertilizer. The increased nitrogen was primarily responsible for greater plant growth as evidenced by higher leaf elongation rate, photosynthetic rate, stem density, and live aboveground biomass. It is well known that nitrogen limits the growth of *Spartina alterniflora*. Fertilizer application also increased soil microbial respiration 8 and 12 weeks after the bioremediation treatment. Increased microbial activity appeared to be responsible for the increased TTAH and alkane degradation. Previous studies (Scherrer and Mille 1990; Lindstrom et al. 1991; Banks and Schwab 1993; Atlas 1995 a and b; Venosa et al. 1996; Lin and Mendelssohn 1998a, 1998b; Lin et al. 1999c, Williams et al. 1999) indicated that fertilization with inorganic nitrogen and phosphorus and organic fertilizer such as poultry litter enhanced degradation of petroleum hydrocarbons. In the present study, fertilizer application may directly enhance soil microbial populations and activity, thus increasing oil degradation. Additionally, fertilizer may increase oil degradation through a phytoremediation effect since fertilization enhanced plant growth, thus potentially promoting oil phytoremediation (Lin and Mendelssohn 1998b). However, in this study we can not separate the effect of fertilizer on oil degradation resulting from increased microbial activity, per se, from that due to plant-induced degradation and uptake.

The soil oxidant treatment had the greatest effect on soil variables and oil degradation rate. The greatest increases in the interstitial phosphorus concentration, soil respiration rate, soil heterotrophic microbial counts, oil-degrading microbial population, and degradation rate of alkane and aromatic hydrocarbons occurred in the treatment receiving soil oxidant and fertilizer compared to the other treatments. Soil respiration measures $CO_2$ release from all living organisms, thus increased soil respiration may be also due to $CO_2$ efflux from plant roots. However, if the increase in soil respiration were primarily caused by an increase in root respiration, the soil respiration in other fertilization treatments (e.g. F+H, F+L and OF+H) would have been expected to increase to a similar extent as the OF+L treatment. In addition, greater soil microbial populations in this treatment support a microbially mediated effect. Soil oxidation status is important for oil degradation (Lin et al., 1997, 1988a: Hambrick et al. 1980). The purpose of the soil oxidant is to oxidize the soil, thus increasing aerobic oil degradation. A handful of studies have reported the enhancements of oil degradation by oxidants although they were not in wetland environments (Lipczynskakochany 1992; Wang and Latchaw 1990; Lovley et al. 1994). The addition of hydrogen peroxide significantly increased degradation of the pollutants, aqueous nitrobenzene and nitrophenols, in a homogeneous phase (Lipczynskakochany 1992). In batch methanogenic cultures, omicron-cresol (phenolic compounds) under high doses of hydrogen peroxide was biodegradable to methane and the biodegradable fraction increased with increasing dose of hydrogen peroxide (Wang, and Latchaw 1990). Lovley et al. (1994) suggest that increasing the bioavailability of Fe(III) by adding suitable ligands provides a potential alternative to oxygen addition for the rapid bioremediation of petroleum-contaminated aquifers.

In the present study, increased oil degradation in the treatment receiving the soil oxidant plus fertilizer was caused by the soil oxidant or the nitrogen and phosphorus fertilizer added with the oxidant. As mentioned in Materials and Methods, in addition to 13.7 g/pot of the soil oxidant (PermeOx), 6.85 g/pot of $KH_2PO_4$ was applied to this treatment to buffer the high pH of the PermeOx. The applied $KH_2PO_4$ in the soil oxidant treatment is equivalent to application of 253 kg P/ha, almost 10-fold higher than the amount of phosphorus contained in the fertilizer (Customblen) treatment. Thus, the higher oil degradation may also be due to the applied phosphorus contained in the pH buffer $KH_2PO_4$. Wright et al. (1997) reported that the addition of phosphorus and nitrogen in a mesocosm experiment significantly increased oil degradation, but nitrogen alone did not. This suggests that phosphorus may limit microbial degradation of oil in some wetlands. In the present study, interstitial phosphorus concentration was about 0.1 ppm in the control. This low phosphorus concentration may limit microbial activity. Application of the pH buffer $KH_2PO_4$ increased interstitial P to about 3 ppm (30-fold higher than the control), and thus may have enhanced microbial oil degradation. Other evidence also suggests that the increased oil degradation was not due to the soil oxidant. Soil oxidant application did not increase the redox potential in this experiment. In addition, heterotrophic microbial populations increased immediately after the oxidant treatment in both flooded and drained conditions. The soil in the drained inundation regime was quite oxidized. The soil oxidant did not increase soil redox potential above that in other drained treatments, indicating that something other than the soil oxidant may have played a role in enhancing microbial counts. The addition of $KH_2PO_4$ with the oxidant was most likely the cause. Maki et al. (1999) also reported sharp increases in bacterial number and the oxygen consumption immediately after addition of sludge containing high concentrations of phosphorus.

Microbial seeding did not significantly affect the marsh plants, soil variables, or oil degradation. Interstitial nitrogen and phosphorus concentrations were quite low in the control and microbial seeding treatments. Microbial seeding did not increase soil fertility, and did not affect plant response. Addition of microbial populations did not significantly increase the microbial counts nor the activity of the soil microbes and oil degradation rate. Previous studies have indicated controversial results of microbial inoculum on bioremediation. Jorgensen et al. (2000) reported no particular effect of added inoculum for soil microbial respiration and oil degradation in a field investigation of bioremediation of diesel-contaminated soil. In a review paper, Atlas (1995b) concluded that although seeding with adapted non-indigenous microbial hydrocarbon degraders has been tested on smaller spills, bioremediation to remove petroleum pollutants by microbial seeding has yet to be demonstrated as efficacious in field trials. However, in a bench-top scale experiment, Cassidy et al. (1997) showed that microbial seeding encapsulated in kappa-carrageenan can enhance pollutant mineralization in a chemically contaminated soil containing pentachlorophenol and petroleum hydrocarbons, but native cells did not. In the present study, microbial seeding may have had no effect due to the natural prevalence of microbes in wetlands or due to the low inorganic nutrient concentrations in the soil, limiting inoculum activity in this study.

**Summary**

Efficacy of bioremediation varied with the different agents applied. Fertilization significantly enhanced plant growth in the treatments receiving fertilizer and the soil oxidant plus fertilizer, but microbial seeding did not affect plant growth. Oil application and inundation regime did not affect growth of S. alterniflora. More importantly, bioremediation with the soil oxidant plus fertilizer combined with the pH buffer, $KH_2PO_4$, significantly affected soil nutrient concentrations, soil microbes, and oil degradation rate, especially in the drained condition. However, the effect of soil oxidant cannot be clearly separated in the present study from the effects of extra phosphorus contained in the pH buffer of $KH_2PO_4$. A future experiment will be designed to determine the role of soil oxidant and phosphorus in bioremediation. Fertilizer application also significantly increased oil degradation. The effect may be due to the fertilizer itself or through a phytoremediation effect; this needs further investigation. Microbial seeding did not significantly affect the plant, soil microbes, or oil degradation, but the low soil nutrient concentrations may have limited the inoculated microbial seeding activity. Future research should investigate the microbial inoculum in a higher fertility soil environment before eliminating its application for bioremediation in the marsh environments. In addition, inundation regime affected bioremediation. Oil degradation was greater in the drained condition than in the flooded condition. The current study shows the potential of bioremediation for oil spill cleanup in coastal wetlands.

# CHAPTER 3

## EFFECTS OF BIOREMEDIATION AGENTS ON OIL DEGRADATION ON MINERAL AND SANDY SALT MARSH SEDIMENTS

by Qianxin Lin, Irving A. Mendelssohn, Charles B. Henry, Jr., Edward B. Overton,
Ralph J. Portier, Paulene O. Roberts, and Maud M. Walsh

Microbial products, cultured and selected to enhance oil degradation rates, have great uncertainties, especially in systems such as wetlands where hydrocarbon degrading bacteria are naturally prevalent (see Introduction for a background discussion). For example, a microbial product used in an experimental mode to test its effectiveness in oil spill cleanup in a marsh in Galveston Bay did not significantly enhance oil degradation (Mearns 1991). Also, two microbial products, which exhibited enhanced biodegradation of Alaska North Slope crude oil in shaker flask tests, did not accelerate biodegradation in a field experiment conducted on an oiled beach in Prince William Sound, although the high variability in the data, the highly weathered nature of the oil, and a lack of sufficient time for biodegradation were cited as possible reasons for the lack of response (Venosa et al. 1992). In a more recent study, Venosa et al. (1996) found that an indigenous microbial inoculum did not increase oil biodegradation in a beach environment. Regardless of these equivocal results, many microbial products have been commercialized. If added microbes, per se, are not effective in increasing oil degradation, the high costs of microbial amendments may not be warranted. Recently, Wright et al. (1997) reported that the addition of phosphorus and nitrogen in a mesocosm experiment significantly increased oil degradation, but nitrogen alone did not. However, comparisons of the effectiveness of different bioremediation agents in wetland environments, based on oil chemical analyses that can identify enhanced biodegradation, are depauperate in the published literature.

Soil oxidation state is another important factor influencing oil biodegradation in wetland environments. Generally, wetland soils are saturated with water and exhibit biochemically reduced soil conditions, which inhibit oil degradation (Hambrick et al. 1980). Therefore, procedures that increase the oxidation status of sediments may favor bioremediation (Lin and Mendelssohn 1997). The use of soil oxidants to increase oil biodegradation in the wetland environment has received little attention (McKee and Mendelssohn 1995).

We initiated a multi-disciplinary investigation to address the question: Is bioremediation, via fertilization, microbial seeding or soil oxidant application, an effective and ecologically safe means of oil spill cleanup in coastal wetlands? Our overall goal was to determine the potential for the use of bioremediation as an oil-spill cleanup technique in wetlands. Specifically, we determined the effects of fertilization, microbial seeding and soil oxidant application on (Hershner and Lake 1977) petroleum hydrocarbon degradation, (Lee et al. 1981) the extent to which the effectiveness of these products is modified by marsh soil type, and (Alexander and Webb 1987) the adverse impacts, if any, of these bioremediation agents on wetland vegetation and microbial activity.

## Materials and Methods

### Marsh Sod

Thirty mineral marsh sods (soil and intact vegetation), approximately 28 cm in diameter (0.062 $m^2$) and 25 cm deep, were extracted from the inland zone (approximately 5-10 m from the creekbank natural levee) of a *Spartina alterniflora*- dominated salt marsh located west of Cocodrie, Louisiana. In addition, 30 sods of the same size were collected from a sandy backbarrier marsh dominated by *S. alterniflora* located approximately 100 meters from the shoreline of the Gulf of Mexico near Fourchon, Louisiana. All 30 sods from each marsh type had similar plant biomasses. Marsh sods from the inland zone were chosen because the inland zone comprises the largest aerial extent of most salt marshes, and is generally of relatively high mineral and organic content. In contrast, the backbarrier marsh is sandy and of low mineral and organic content. The mineral marsh soil was composed of 63.8% clay, 31% silt and 5.2% fine sand, with 18.6% soil organic matter and 0.312 $g/cm^3$ soil bulk density. The sandy marsh soil was composed of 2.5% clay, 6.3% silt and 91.2% fine sand, with 0.5% soil organic matter and 1.35 $g/cm^3$ soil bulk density. We recognize that soil types will likely influence bioremediation, and, thus, this factor was examined in this research. *Spartina alterniflora* is the dominant intertidal salt marsh grass along the Atlantic and Gulf Coasts of the United States, and results from this study should be generally applicable to many other salt marshes.

## Experimental Design

In the greenhouse, artificially weathered Louisiana crude oil (25% weathered by volume) was applied at a dose of 2 $L/m^2$ (2 mm oil thickness) to the surface of all experimental units (marsh sods in 28 cm x 32 cm buckets fitted with water level controls). After the applied oil was evenly spread over the surface water in the buckets, the water was drained from the bottom of the buckets to allow the oil to come in contact with and penetrate the soil of each sod. The initial oil concentration in the top 5 cm of soil after the application of the oil was 20.8 mg/g dry soil (s.e. 0.85) in the sandy sediment and 57.9 mg/g dry soil (s.e. 9.7) in the mineral sediment as determined by the gravimetric method with dichloromethane (DCM) extraction (Lin and Mendelssohn 1996). The difference in the initial oil concentration between two types of sediment was primarily due to their different soil bulk densities. The oil was artificially weathered to remove hydrocarbons nC-10 and below, thereby simulating oil spilled in open water and subsequently transported into a salt marsh by winds or tides. The following treatments were randomly assigned to both mineral and sandy marsh sods with applied oil: (1) slow release fertilizer, (2) microbial seeding plus slow release fertilizer, (3) soil oxidant, (4) soil oxidant plus slow release fertilizer, (5) soluble fertilizer, and (6) control (no application of products). The experimental design was a randomized block by the location within greenhouse with a 6 x 2 factorial treatment arrangement (the six bioremediation types mentioned above and two soil types—mineral and sandy). Each treatment combination was replicated five times for a total of 60 marsh sods. Statistical analysis was conducted with the SAS system (SAS 1990). General Linear Model (GLM) was used to test for statistically significant differences ($P<0.05$) among the treatments, and Duncan's multiple range test was used to determine significant differences among the main factors. Treatment-level combination differences, if interactions of main factors were significant, were tested with least square means.

## Experimental Procedures

The products were applied to the soil surface in a manner similar to that during a field application and following the manufacturer's specifications. Slow release fertilizer (Osmocote 14-14-14, product of Grace Sierra, Milpitas, CA) was applied at the rate of 93 $g/m^2$ each application (130 kg N as $NH_4$ and $NO_3$, 57 kg P as $P_2O_5$ and 108 kg K as $K_2O$ per hectare). The microbial product (Petrobac, selected for hydrocarbon degradation in a saline medium, a product of Polybac Corp., Bethlehem, PA) was applied at the rate of 0.833 $L/m^2$ of inoculum (46 g of Petrobac/L of deionized water). A soil oxidant (PermeOx, a product of FMC Corp., Philadelphia, PA) was applied at the rate of 111 $g/m^2$. All products were applied 3 times (i.e., at days 0, 40, and 80 after application of oil) during the low tide over a 4-month experimental period (8/96-12/96). The soluble fertilizer treatment ($NH_4NO_3$ and $NaH_2PO_4$) was implemented by applying nitrogen and/or phosphorus to maintain concentrations above 5 ppm in the interstitial water throughout the experiment to insure high and likely non-limiting concentrations for bioremediation. Semi-quantitative measurements of ammonium, nitrate and phosphate (CHEMets Kit, products of CHEMetrics, Inc., Calverton, VA) were used weekly to determine when application of soluble fertilizer was needed. Also, quantitative determinations of ammonium, nitrate and phosphate were conducted as described below. Water levels were manipulated to simulate a diurnal tide regime with 12 hours of night-time high tide (5-cm deep surface water) and 12 hours of day-time low tide (water drained from the bottom of the pots to individual reservoirs and reused to create high tide). Tapwater was used to replace evapotranspirational water loss.

Plant and Soil Responses

*Aboveground Biomass of Dominant Marsh Plants.* Plant aboveground biomass was analyzed at the end of a four-month experimental period to determine the effect, if any, of product addition on plant growth. Plant aboveground material was clipped at the soil surface. Live and dead components were separated, dried in a oven at 65°C to constant weight, and weighed.

*Soil Respiration Rate.* In-situ measurement of soil respiration rate, an indicator of soil microbial activity, was conducted with an ADC (the Analytical Development Co. LTD) infra-red gas analyzer (IRGA) by measuring carbon dioxide production from soil. A PVC chamber (4 cm in diameter and 8 cm in height) with one open end was equipped with an inlet and an outlet for air flow through the chamber. The open end of the chamber was inserted into the soil 4 cm below the soil surface. An air flow rate through the chamber was held constant at 300 ml per minute by an ADC mass flow controller. The respiratory $CO_2$ produced from the soil resulted in a difference in $CO_2$ concentration between inlet and outlet that was measured by an ADC infra-red gas analyzer. Soil respiration was calculated based on the $CO_2$ exchange rate from the soil per unit surface.

*Soil Redox Potential.* Soil redox potentials at 2 and 10 cm depths were determined with bright platinum electrodes and a calomel reference electrode. Readings were taken with a portable pH/mV digital meter. The potential of a calomel reference electrode (+244 mV) was added to each value to calculate Eh (Patrick *et al.*, 1996).

*Soil Nutrient Concentrations.* Interstitial water samples were withdrawn from soil sods with a simple apparatus as described by McKee et al. (1988). This consisted of a small diameter (3 mm inside diameter) rigid plastic tube, containing numerous 0.5 mm diameter holes covered with 3 to 4 layers of cheesecloth, connected to a 30 ml syringe. The collected interstitial water was filtered through a 0.45 μ syringe filter. Inorganic nutrients in the filtered interstitial water were analyzed to determine the effect of product application on soil fertility and other variables. Ammonium-nitrogen ($NH_4$) and nitrate-nitrogen ($NO_3 + NO_2$) were analyzed with an auto-analyzer before and two weeks after the third product application. Nutrient levels were analyzed at these specific times to determine to what extent available nutrients were depleted before the next nutrient application and whether the nutrient levels remained high after addition (over a two-week period). Total inorganic nitrogen was determined as the sum of $NH_4$, $NO_3$, and $NO_2$-nitrogen concentrations. Phosphorus and potassium concentrations in the interstitial water were analyzed with ICP (inductively coupled argon-plasma emission spectrometer). Phosphate concentrations were estimated from regression equations relating ICP phosphorus to methylene blue determined phosphate measured in a subset of marsh sods (Y = 1.195x-0.718; $r^2$=0.996; n=20).

*Microbial Populations.* The top 5 cm of the soil in each sod was collected for oil chemistry and microbial analyses. Heterotrophic bacterial populations and petroleum-degrading organisms were enumerated to determine the relationship between microbes and oil degradation. Soils for microbial analyses were subsampled from thoroughly mixed surface soil samples. Standard plate counts were performed according to the method described in Wollum (1982). Approximately 1.25 g of sample was added to 99 ml of normal saline (0.85 weight % NaCl). Several drops of sterile Tween 80 were added as a surfactant. The bottles were mixed on a vortex mixer, then shaken vigorously. Subsequent serial dilutions in 99 ml of normal saline were made up to $10^{-6}$ g/ml dilution and plated by the pour plate method. Nutrient agar (Difco) was used to grow general heterotrophic bacteria. A minimal salt agar to which 50 ppm kerosene was added as the sole carbon source was used for the selective culturing for petroleum-degrading organisms. Plates were incubated at 30°C for 24-26 hours, then colony-forming units of bacteria were enumerated. Values were calculated for colony-forming units/g dry weight of soil.

*Residual Oil Chemistry in the Soil.* The top 5 cm of soil from each sod was collected, thoroughly homogenized, subsampled and extracted using a modified EPA method 3550. Approximately 20 grams of wet sediment were extracted using dichloromethane and sodium sulfate as a chemical drying agent (Venosa et al. 1996; Sauer and Boehm 1993; Henry and Overton 1993; Henry et al. 1993), then reduced to a final volume of 10 ml. A field treatment composite was then analyzed by gas chromatography-mass spectrometry (GC/MS) operated in the Selective Ion Monitoring (SIM) Mode to characterize compositional changes in selected aromatic hydrocarbons (AH) and normal hydrocarbons (NH). Although these selected targeted AH generally represent less than 5% of the bulk oil composition, they are essential to characterize petroleum source, identify potential biological effects, determine exposure pathways, and monitor weathering trends and degradation of the oil (Sauer and Boehm 1991; Roques et al. 1994). The targeted aromatic hydrocarbons are listed in Table 9.

**Results**

**Plant Growth Response**

The effect of the bioremediation products on the growth response of the salt marsh grass *Spartina alterniflora* was assessed by determining aboveground biomass. Fertilizer had a positive effect on aboveground biomass (Fig. 40) regardless of soil type (no significant treatment by soil type interaction) with live aboveground biomass significantly higher (p <0.0001) in the treatment receiving soluble fertilizer than without. Live aboveground biomass of *S. alterniflora* in all treatments receiving slow release fertilizer tended to be greater than that without fertilizer, but differences were not statistically significant. As expected, application of the microbial product had no significant effect on plant growth response; live aboveground biomass in the microbial product plus fertilizer treatment was not significantly different from that receiving fertilizer alone. Also, application of the soil oxidant had no significant effect on plant growth. Live aboveground biomass in the treatment receiving the soil oxidant alone was not significantly different from the control, and live aboveground biomass in the treatment receiving the soil oxidant plus fertilizer was not significantly different than that receiving fertilizer alone. Dead and total aboveground biomass did not significantly differ with product application, and there was no significant difference in aboveground biomass between marsh types.

Table 9.    Target Compounds Assessed by GC/MS

| Compound | *ion* mass | Compound | *ion* mass | Compound | *ion* mass |
|---|---|---|---|---|---|
| alkanes* (nC-10 thru nC-31) | 85 | C-3 fluorenes | 208 | fluoranthrene/pyrene | 202 |
| decalin* | 138 | dibenzothiophene | 184 | C-1 pyrenes | 216 |
| C-1 decalin* | 152 | C-1 dibenzothiophenes | 198 | C-2 pyrenes | 230 |
| C-2 decalin* | 166 | C-2 dibenzothiophenes | 212 | chrysene | 228 |
| C-3 decalin* | 180 | C-3 dibenzothiophenes | 226 | C-1 chrysenes | 242 |
| naphthalene | 128 | phenanthrene | 178 | C-2 chrysenes | 256 |
| C-1 naphthalenes | 142 | C-1 phenanthrenes | 192 | benzo(b)fluoranthene | 252 |
| C-2 naphthalenes | 156 | C-2 phenanthrenes | 206 | benzo(k)fluoranthene | 252 |
| C-3 naphthalenes | 170 | C-3 phenanthrenes | 220 | benzo(e)pyrene | 252 |
| C-4 naphthalenes | 184 | naphthobenzothiophene | 234 | benzo(a)pyrene | 252 |
| fluorene | 166 | C-1 naphthobenzothiophenes | 248 | perylene | 252 |
| C-1 fluorenes | 180 | C-2 naphthobenzothiophenes | 262 | indeno(1,2,3-cd)pyrene | 276 |
| C-2 fluorenes | 194 | C-3 naphthobenzothiophenes | 276 | sterenes (217 family)* | 217 |
| dibenzo(a,h)anthracene | 278 | benzo(g,h,i)perylene | 276 | hopanes (191 family)* | 191 |

Sum of these compounds excluding those identified with a * is the TTAH value.

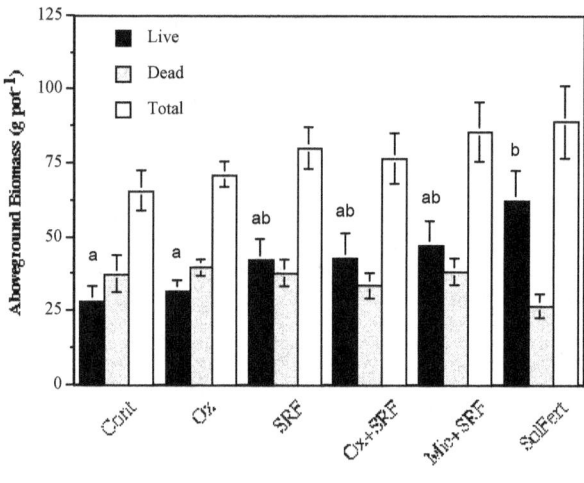

BIOREMEDIATION AGENTS

Figure 40. The effect of bioremediation products on aboveground biomass *of Spartina alterniflora*, averaged over marsh type, after a 4-month experimental period (n=10, means ± standard errors). Means with the same letter are not significantly different within each biomass component; for example, means with the letter a are significantly different from means with the letters bc, but not from means with the letters ab. Cont: control; Ox: soil oxidant; SRF: slow release fertilizer; Ox+SRF: soil oxidant plus slow release fertilizer; Mic+SRF: microbial agent plus slow release fertilizer; SolFert: soluble fertilizer.

## Microbial Response

In-situ soil respiration was measured to identify if the application of the bioremediation agents affected the metabolism of the soil microbial community. The fertilizer treatments had significant positive effects on soil respiration compared to those treatments without fertilizer for both soil types (Fig. 41, no significant treatment by soil type interaction). However, addition of the microbial product or the soil oxidant had no significant effect on soil respiration. Soil respiration rates of the treatment receiving microbial seeding plus slow release fertilizer was not significantly different from that of the fertilizer alone (Fig. 41), suggesting that the microbial agent had no effect on soil respiration. Soil respiration rates of the treatments receiving the soil oxidant alone and the soil oxidant plus fertilizer were also not significantly different from those of the control and fertilizer alone, respectively (Fig. 41). Overall, soil respiration was significantly higher for the sandy soil (7.04 $\mu$mol/m$^{2/}$s $\pm$ 0.54 s.e., n=30) than for the mineral marsh soil (5.9 $\mu$mol/m$^{2/}$s $\pm$ 0.33 s.e, n=30).

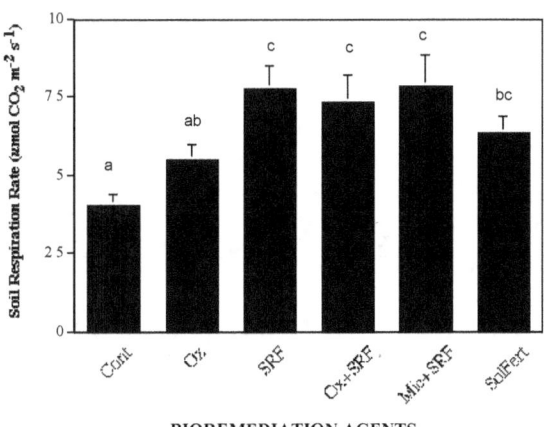

Figure 41. Soil microbial respiration responses, averaged over marsh type, to bioremediation product treatments 7 weeks after application (n=10, mean ± s.e). Means with the same letter are not significantly different. Cont: control; Ox: soil oxidant; SRF: slow release fertilizer; Ox+SRF: soil oxidant plus slow release fertilizer; Mic+SRF: microbial agent plus slow release fertilizer; SolFert: soluble fertilizer.

Soil microbial response was also evaluated by determining the colony-forming units of heterotrophic bacteria and petroleum-degrading organisms (Table 10). Fertilizer application tended to increase the populations of heterotrophic bacteria (Table 10), which is likely correlated to increased microbial degradation of residual oil. However, the differences in heterotrophic bacterial numbers between the treatments with and without fertilizer were not statistically significant (p=0.39) because of large within-treatment variation. The application of the microbial product and the soil oxidant had no significant effects on heterotrophic bacterial numbers. Similar trends were observed for petroleum-degrading organisms, with no significant difference among product treatments (p=0.35) (Table 10). Heterotrophic bacterial numbers (p=0.1) and petroleum-degrading organisms (p=0.308) did not significantly differ between soil type, thus means are averages over the two soil types (Table 10).

Table 10. Effect of Bioremediation Products on Soil Heterotrophic Populations and Petroleum Degraders After a 4-Month Experimental Period

|  | Cont | Ox | SRF | Ox+SRF | Mic+SRF | SolFert |
|---|---|---|---|---|---|---|
| Hetero-bacteria | $1.76 \times 10^8$ $(3.49 \times 10^7)$ | $3.76 \times 10^7$ $(1.09 \times 10^7)$ | $1.60 \times 10^9$ $(1.16 \times 10^9)$ | $2.92 \times 10^9$ $(1.04 \times 10^9)$ | $4.92 \times 10^9$ $(4.1 \times 10^9)$ | $1.44 \times 10^9$ $(5.43 \times 10^8)$ |
| Petro-degrader | $3.32 \times 10^8$ $(1.98 \times 10^8)$ | $2.28 \times 10^7$ $(1.46 \times 10^7)$ | $7.15 \times 10^7$ $(2.69 \times 10^7)$ | $4.48 \times 10^9$ $(3.99 \times 10^9)$ | $1.92 \times 10^8$ $(1.06 \times 10^8)$ | $2.29 \times 10^8$ $(1.26 \times 10^8)$ |

Cont: control; Ox: soil oxidant; SRF: slow release fertilizer; Ox+SRF: soil oxidant plus slow release fertilizer; Mic+SRF: microbial agent plus slow release fertilizer; SolFert: soluble fertilizer. Values Are Means (the colony-forming units/g dry soil), averaged over the two soil types, with standard errors in parentheses (n=10).

## Soil Fertility

The effect of fertilizer addition on soil fertility was determined by analyzing the concentrations of inorganic nutrients in the soil interstitial water. The application of soluble fertilizer significantly ($p<0.0001$) increased the concentrations of ammonium, nitrate and phosphate in the interstitial water (Table 11). The ammonium, nitrate and total inorganic nitrogen concentrations tended to be higher in all treatments with slow release fertilizer than without, but the differences were not statistically significant. Marsh types did not affect the interstitial nitrogen concentration. The interstitial phosphate concentration (Table 11) was significantly higher in treatments with fertilizer than without ($p<0.0001$) and higher in the sandy soil type than in the mineral soil ($p<0.0001$). A significant interaction ($p<0.0001$) between product treatment and soil type indicated that fertilizer application increased interstitial phosphate concentration more in the sandy soil than in mineral soils. Potassium concentration did not significantly vary among bioremediation treatments.

Table 11.  Effect of Bioremediation Products on the Inorganic Interstitial Nutrient Concentrations Before and 2 Weeks After the Third Product Application.

| Nutrients | Mineral Marsh | | | | | | Sandy Marsh | | | | | |
|---|---|---|---|---|---|---|---|---|---|---|---|---|
| | Cont | Ox | SRF | O+F | M+F | SF | Cont | Ox | SRF | O+F | M+F | SF |
| NH4 | 0.07 | 0.09 | 0.47 | 0.34 | 0.17 | 5.66* | 0.06 | 0.07 | 0.43 | 0.11 | 0.21 | 5.82* |
| | (0.03) | (0.05) | (0.18) | (0.16) | (0.07) | (0.67) | (0.01) | (0.02) | (0.13) | (0.03) | (0.12) | (1.85) |
| NO3 | 0.10 | 0.05 | 0.13 | 0.04 | 0.11 | 2.35* | 0.11 | 0.10 | 0.06 | 0.18 | 0.13 | 1.42* |
| | (0.01) | (0.01) | (0.03) | (0.01) | (0.03) | (1.22) | (0.01) | (0.02) | (0.02) | (0.04) | (0.06) | (1.04) |
| Total inorganic N | 0.17 | 0.147 | 0.60 | 0.38 | 0.28 | 8.01* | 0.17 | 0.17 | 0.50 | 0.29 | 0.34 | 7.32* |
| | (0.05) | (0.06) | (0.20) | (0.15) | (0.09) | (1.75) | (0.02) | (0.02) | (0.15) | (0.06) | (0.18) | (2.68) |
| PO4 | 0.44 | 0.40 | 1.245* | 1.96* | 1.23* | 1.75* | 0.67 | 0.34 | 9.60* | 4.12* | 11.2* | 20.25* |
| | (0.04) | (0.06) | (0.26) | (0.36) | (0.24) | (0.32) | (0.14) | (0.12) | (1.47) | (1.02) | (2.31) | (5.91) |

Values are means (ppm), averaged over the two sampling events, with standard errors in parentheses (n=5). Cont: control; Ox: soil oxidant; SRF: slow release fertilizer; O+F: soil oxidant plus slow release fertilizer; M+F: microbial agent plus slow release fertilizer; SF: Soluble fertilizer. Values with asterisks (*) are significantly higher than their controls.

## Oil Biodegradation

In general, fertilizer application enhanced oil biodegradation in the soil. The concentrations of both total targeted normal hydrocarbons (TTNH) and total targeted aromatic hydrocarbons (TTAH) remaining in the soil were significantly reduced ($p<0.0001$) by all remediation treatments receiving the fertilizer application (Figs. 42 and 43), Table 12. Concentration of TTNH remaining in marsh soils of the treatments receiving fertilizer was only 16% of those without fertilizer (averaged over all fertilizer treatments). Concentration of TTNH remaining in sandy soil was significantly higher ($p<0.0001$) than in mineral soil, with 177 µg/g dry soil ($\pm$ 35, n = 30) in the former versus the latter. A significant interaction ($p<0.0001$) between product addition and marsh type indicated that the soil oxidant addition in the mineral soil appeared to have an adverse effect on TTNH degradation as evidenced by higher TTNH concentrations with the soil oxidant compared to the control in the mineral soil, and no difference in the sandy soil. Also, soil type significantly affected the percentage of fertilizer-enhanced degradation of TTNH (Table 12) compared to the control (mineral soil: 26% $\pm$ 5 (n=20), averaged over treatments receiving fertilizer relative to the mean of the mineral control; sandy soil: 13% $\pm$ 3, n=20), suggesting that fertilizer application was more effective in enhancing TTNH degradation in the sandy soil than in the mineral soil.

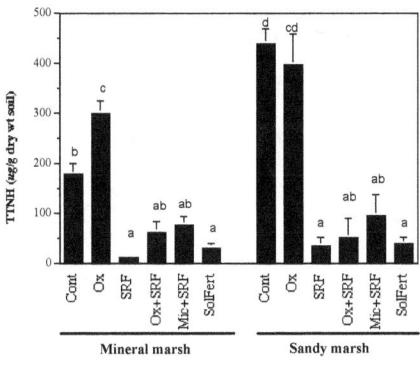

Figure 42. Effect of the bioremediation products on total targeted normal hydrocarbons (TTNH) (n=5, mean ± s.e). Means with the same letter are not significantly different. Cont: control; Ox: soil oxidant; SRF: slow release fertilizer; Ox+SRF: soil oxidant plus slow release fertilizer; Mic+SRF: microbial agent plus slow release fertilizer; SolFert: soluble fertilizer.

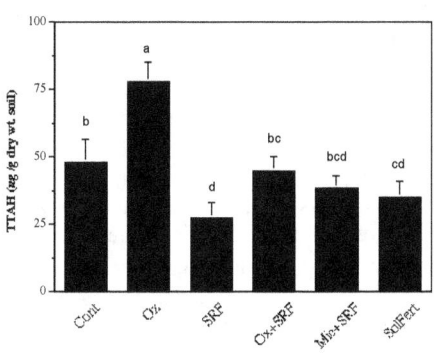

Figure 43. Total targeted aromatic hydrocarbons (TTAH) remaining in the soil, averaged over marsh type, as a function of the bioremediation product treatments (n=10, mean ± s.e.). Means with the same letter are not significantly different. Cont: control; Ox: soil oxidant; SRF: slow release fertilizer; Ox+SRF: soil oxidant plus slow release fertilizer; Mic+SRF: microbial agent plus slow release fertilizer; SolFert: soluble fertilizer.

Table 12. Effect of Bioremediation Product Application on Relative Oil Degradation, the Percentage Decrease of Petroleum Components Normalized to Each Soil Type's Control (Control 100%).

| | Mineral Marsh | | | | | | Sandy Marsh | | | | | |
|---|---|---|---|---|---|---|---|---|---|---|---|---|
| | Cont | Ox | SRF | O+F | M+F | SF | Cont | Ox | SRF | O+F | M+F | SF |
| TTNH | 100[b] | 167[a] | 7[c] | 36[c] | 43[c] | 18[c] | 100[b] | 90[b] | 8[c] | 12[c] | 22[c] | 9[c] |
| | (11.1) | (14) | (2) | (11) | (10) | (5) | (7) | (14) | (4) | (9) | (10) | (3) |
| TTAH | 100[bc] | 271[a] | 54[c] | 138[b] | 123[bc] | 83[bc] | 100[bc] | 123[bc] | 58[c] | 77[bc] | 66[c] | 70[c] |
| | (15) | (30) | (14) | (16) | (14) | (14) | (5) | (16) | (8) | (12) | (80) | (8) |

| | Cont | Ox | SRF | O+F | M+F | SF |
|---|---|---|---|---|---|---|
| TTNH/ | 100[a] | 78[a] | 10[b] | 14[b] | 22[b] | 11[b] |
| Hopane | (6) | (8) | (3) | (4) | (4) | (2) |
| TTAH/ | 100[a] | 115[a] | 60[b] | 69[b] | 66[b] | 64[b] |
| Hopane | (4) | (9) | (5) | (3) | (3) | (4) |

Values are means (% of the control) with standard errors in parentheses (n=5 for TTNH and TTAH, n=10 for TTNH/Hopane and TTAH/Hopane, averaged over marsh type). Values lower than 100% indicate enhanced biodegradation, and values higher than 100% indicate inhibited biodegradation. Cont: control; Ox: soil oxidant; SRF: slow release fertilizer; O+F: soil oxidant plus slow release fertilizer; M+F: microbial agent plus slow release fertilizer; SF: Soluble fertilizer. Means with the same letter are not significantly different within each hydrocarbon component.

Bioremediation product application significantly ($p<0.0001$) affected TTAH concentrations in the sediments (Fig. 12). Concentrations of TTAH remaining in marsh soils receiving fertilizer were 57% lower than those without fertilizer (averaged over all fertilizer treatments vs. no fertilizer treatments). TTAH concentrations in the treatments receiving slow release fertilizer and soluble fertilizer were significantly lower than the control. In addition, TTAH concentration in the sandy substrate was significantly higher than in mineral substrate, with 59 μg/g dry soil (± 4, n=30) in the former and 32 μg/g dry soil (± 4, n=30) in the latter. TTAH concentrations in the treatments receiving the soil oxidant alone were significantly higher than that of the control. Also, soil type significantly affected the percentage of fertilizer-enhanced degradation of TTAH (Table 12) compared to the control (mineral soil: 99% ± 10% [n=20], averaged over treatments receiving fertilizer relative to the mean of the mineral control; sandy soil: 68% ± 4 [n=20]), suggesting that the fertilizer application was more effective in enhancing TTAH degradation in the sandy soil than in the mineral soil.

The TTNH/Hopane and TTAH/Hopane ratios were consistently significantly lower ($p<0.0001$) in the treatments with fertilizer than without, supporting the conclusion of a fertilizer-enhanced biodegradation (Table 12). In addition, the percentage change of TTNH/Hopane and TTNH/Hopane for the fertilizer treatments compared to the control's (Table 12) showed no effects of the microbial product and the soil oxidant. However, a fertilizer effect on oil biodegradation was evident. Overall, the addition of the microbial product did not significantly lower the values of TTNH, TTAH, TTNH/Hopane and TTAH/Hopane in the soil relative to controls (Figs. 42 and 43, Table 12). Also, the soil oxidant did not significantly affect the values of TTNH, TTAH, TTNH/Hopane and TTAH/Hopane in the soil relative to controls except with the increase in TTNH and TTAH in the mineral soil by the soil oxidant compared to the control.

**Discussion**

Biostimulation, the enhancement of biodegradation by increasing indigenous microbial activity, was demonstrated in both mineral and sandy marsh sods with concurrent stimulation in microbial activity and plant growth with fertilizer addition (a type of biostimulation). In contrast, microbial seeding (bioaugmentation) and soil oxidant application (a type of biostimulation) had no positive effect on plant growth, microbial activity, or petroleum hydrocarbon degradation.

Application of fertilizer increased live aboveground biomass, especially in the treatment receiving the soluble fertilizer. Salt marshes are usually deficient in inorganic nutrients (Wilsey et al. 1992). The application of fertilizer provided essential macronutrients (N and P) to marsh plants. As a result, plants were visually more vigorous and had higher live aboveground biomass in the treatments with fertilizer than without. When this experiment started in August, the marsh plants in the sods had almost reached their peak biomass. Little aboveground growth occurred during the following 4-month experimental period. Thus, biomass differences between fertilizer and non-fertilizer treatments were not great. It is not surprising that the microbial product had no significant effect on plant growth because it only contained cultured bacteria, with no inorganic nutrients. Also, the soil oxidant elicited no positive effect on plant growth, suggesting that soil oxygen availability was not limiting plant growth. Because the inundation regime in this experiment was 12-hours drained and 12-hours flooded every 24-hour period, the sods were relatively aerobic (average soil redox potential (Eh) of +121 mV at the depth of 2 cm below the soil surface and +31 mV at 10 cm depth even when flooded). Also, the soil oxidant did not significantly increase soil Eh relative to control. Thus, the application of the soil oxidant had no measurable effect on soil oxidation status. The Eh level in this experiment was not low enough to stress *S. alterniflora*, which adapts to flooding with a well-developed aerenchyma system that ventilates the roots with air. *Spartina alterniflora* can grow vigorously under moderately reducing condition (Mendelssohn and McKee 1987).

Microbial activity was enhanced by bioremediation as evidenced by increased soil respiration. The living soil community is composed of bacteria, fungi, invertebrates and roots of *S. alterniflora*. The greater soil respiration with fertilization could have resulted from an increase in microbial activity, from enhanced root biomass and root respiration, or from both. However, our on-going studies show no significant relationship between the mass of living roots of *S. alterniflora* and the soil respiration rate ($r^2$=0.03, p=0.802). Therefore, the fertilizer-induced increase in soil respiration was most likely due to increased soil microbial activity. This conclusion is also supported by the heterotrophic bacteria data, showing an increase, albeit not significant, in colony counts with fertilization. A number of studies have demonstrated the effects of inorganic nutrient addition on microbial activity and population counts. In the Exxon Valdes oil spill, fertilizer application increased microbial number and activity (Chianelli et al. 1991), and fertilizer application increased the populations of alkane and aromatic degraders in an experimental oil spill in Delaware beach (Venosa et al. 1996). Microbial population and activity were also enhanced by nutrient addition to laboratory microcosms containing hydrocarbon-contaminated arctic soils (Braddock et al. 1997).

Soil inorganic nutrient concentrations were increased by fertilizer application, especially by the soluble nutrient addition. The objective of the soluble fertilizer treatment was to maintain elevated interstitial nutrient levels with nutrient additions when needed on a weekly-basis. This objective was met. The interstitial nitrogen concentrations in the treatments receiving slow release fertilizer tended to be higher than that without fertilizer although the difference was not statistically significant. In a comparison of bioremediation with and without marsh plants, fertilizer application did not increase the interstitial nitrogen pools when marsh plants were present, but significantly increased nitrogen concentrations in the absence of plants (Lin and Mendelssohn 1997). Thus, plant uptake can regulate the interstitial nitrogen concentration levels. Therefore, soil nitrogen pools cannot solely be used as indicators of fertilizer application rate during bioremediation trials when plants are present. The fertilizer applications also significantly raised phosphate concentrations compared to the control, with greater increase in the sandy marsh sediment than in the more mineral soil.

Fertilizer application changed the soil environment by increasing nutrient concentrations and microbial activity, responses that should favor oil biodegradation. The concentrations of TTNH and TTAH in both types of marsh sediments with fertilizer application were significantly lower than without fertilizer application. The extent that fertilizer enhanced the reduction in TTNH concentration over no-fertilizer was much greater than for TTAH. For example, the residual TTNH in the sediment receiving slow release fertilizer was only 8% of the control (no bioremediation products added), while the TTAH in the same treatment was 56% of the control, suggesting that TTNH was more biodegradable than TTAH when fertilized. An experimental oil spill on a Delaware beach also found that the degradation rate of alkanes was greater than that for aromatic hydrocarbons (Venosa et al. 1996). Also, nutrient addition stimulated saturate degradation to a greater extent than aromatic degradation under shake-flask conditions (Fedorak and Westlake 1981). In the present study, although interstitial nitrogen and phosphorus concentrations were much higher in treatments receiving soluble fertilizer than in those with slow release fertilizer, the petroleum hydrocarbons (TTNH and TTAH) remaining in the sediment of the former were greater than in the latter. This indicates that maintaining constant and high (7-8 ppm or above) nitrogen and phosphorus concentrations in the interstitial water in this study was not necessary for maximum oil biodegradation. Fertilizer addition to hydrocarbon-contaminated arctic soils showed that high nutrient levels (N>61 ppm and P>106 ppm of dry soil) did not enhance microbial activity and hydrocarbon degradation more than at lower concentrations (22.2

ppm N and 37.6 ppm P) (Braddock et al. 1997). In a mesocosm experiment (Wright et al. 1997), addition of phosphorus and nitrogen significantly increased oil degradation, but nitrogen alone did not. This suggests that phosphorus may limit microbial degradation of oil in some wetlands. In an experiment associated with the Exxon Valdez oil spill (Bragg et al. 1993), effectiveness was determined to depend primarily on the amount of nitrogen fertilizer delivered to the sediment per unit oil present. The effectiveness of nitrogen or phosphorus addition on oil bioremediation most likely depends on their background concentrations and availability in the soil.

Hopane, a saturated, high molecular weight alkane in crude oil, has been shown to be highly resistant to biodegradation and is often used as an internal reference marker for oil biodegradation experiments (Venosa et al. 1996; Atlas 1995). In the present study, when the analytes were normalized to hopane (TTNH/Hopane and TTAH/Hopane), an enhancement of oil biodegradation by fertilizer was also observed. All treatments with fertilizer application had consistently lower ratios of TTNH/Hopane and TTAH/Hopane compared to those without fertilizer. The differences among treatments receiving fertilizer was small, regardless of whether other products (oxidant or microbial agent) were included, further suggesting the importance of fertilization in stimulating oil biodegradation.

The addition of the microbial product to the slow release fertilizer did not affect soil respiration rate, heterotrophic microbial populations, petroleum-degrading microbes, or TTNH and TTAH concentrations in the sediment any more than the application of slow release fertilizer alone. TTNH/hopane and TTAH/hopane ratios further indicated no significant positive effect of microbial seeding on oil biodegradation. Our results suggest that presence of microbial hydrocarbon degraders in Louisiana coastal marshes is not limiting biodegradation. The present study supports a number of other studies showing the ineffectiveness of microbial inoculents on oil biodegradation in wetlands (Mearns 1991; Venosa et al. 1992). Virtually all marine ecosystems harbor indigenous hydrocarbon-degrading microbes. The hydrocarbon degraders, which usually comprise <1% of the bacterial community in unpolluted environments, often exceed 10% following petroleum contamination (Atlas 1993). Thus, microbial seeding usually is not an important limiting factor for oil degradation in wetlands (Prince et al. 1993). This study suggests that the high cost of microbial amendments for oil bioremediation may not be warranted in coastal marshes.

The soil oxidant also did not significantly enhance oil degradation rate in this study. Generally, petroleum biodegradation rate is low in anaerobic sediments because molecular oxygen is required by most microorganisms for the initial step in hydrocarbon metabolism (Atlas 1995). In the present experiment, the marsh sods were drained daily to simulate a diurnal tidal regime. During the 12-hour daily low tide period, interstitial water drained from soil pores and atmospheric air was able to enter the soil via direct diffusion from the soil surface. Thus, the soil was relatively oxidized (+388 mV and +326 mV at 2 and 10 cm below soil surface, respectively) when drained. The effect of direct atmospheric oxygen diffusion into the soil on soil oxidation status likely overwhelmed the relatively minor effect of the soil oxidant. Even during the 12-hour high tide period, the inundation was not long enough to cause severely reducing conditions as mentioned previously. The redox potential was not significantly different between treatments with and without the soil oxidant. Also, interstitial pH was not significantly affected by the soil oxidant or the other product applications (7.7 $\pm$ 0.04, n=120). Interestingly, the soil oxidant appeared to have a negative effect on oil degradation in this experiment when the soil oxidant was applied without fertilizer. TTNH and TTAH in the mineral marsh receiving the soil oxidant alone were significantly higher than those in the control (no product added), but the differences in concentrations of TTNH and TTAH between the treatments receiving the soil oxidant plus slow release fertilizer and slow release fertilizer only were not significantly different (Figs. 42 and 43). However, the TTNH/hopane and TTAH/hopane ratios (Table 12) suggest that the soil oxidant had neither positive nor negative effects on oil biodegradation.

Marsh soil type affected oil biodegradation. In the present study, TTNH, TTAH, TTNH/Hopane and TTAH/Hopane were higher in the sandy marsh than in the mineral marsh soil. The differences in these values were primarily controlled by the no fertilizer treatments (control and soil oxidant alone). Higher TTNH and TTNH/hopane values in the controls of the sandy soil than in the mineral soil may indicate lower natural microbial biodegradation rates in sandy soil than in mineral soil. More importantly, however, the percentage of decrease in TTNH in treatments receiving fertilizer compared to the related control (Table 12) was greater in sandy soil (87%) than in mineral soil (74%), suggesting that biostimulation with fertilizer application was more effective in the former than in the latter, although fertilizer significantly enhanced TTNH biodegradation in both soil types.

## Summary

Oil bioremediation with fertilizer application has shown great potential for oil spill cleanup in coastal marshes in the present study. Inorganic nutrient addition was the most effective bioremediation agent tested in this study. The ambient inorganic nutrient concentrations in the marsh sods, ca. 0.2 ppm nitrogen and 0.5 ppm phosphate in the sediment interstitial water, were not high enough for optimum microbial degradation of petroleum. Fertilizer addition increased soil nutrient concentration and/or availability which, in turn, stimulated soil microbial activity. As a result, fertilizer application significantly increased biodegradation of normal alkane and aromatic hydrocarbons. The concentrations of total targeted normal hydrocarbons remaining in sediments with fertilizer were 26% of the control in the mineral marsh, and 13% of the control in the sandy marsh. For both alkanes and aromatic hydrocarbons, enhanced biodegradation was observed with the hopane normalization method in treatments with fertilizer compared to treatments without fertilizer. However, raising nitrogen (up to 8 ppm) and phosphorus (up to 20 ppm) concentrations above that created with slow release fertilizer did not further increase oil biodegradation. Soil type influenced bioremediation. Fertilizer was more effective in enhancing oil biodegradation in sandy soils than mineral soils; the percentages of TTNH and TTAH remaining in treatments receiving fertilizer compared to controls were lower in sandy than in mineral soils, although natural (unfertilized) degradation rates of TTNH and TTAH may be lower in the sandy soils than in the mineral soils. Microbial seeding and soil oxidant addition did not enhance petroleum biodegradation rates, even when combined with slow release fertilizer, more than that resulting from the slow release fertilizer alone. These results suggest that the high costs of microbial amendments during bioremediation trials may not be warranted in coastal marshes where oil-adapted microbes occur. Although the soil oxidant did not accelerate oil biodegradation, under other experimental conditions or with the application of other oxidants, these products, in combination with fertilizer, may yet prove to be valuable. The results of this investigation indicate that bioremediation with fertilizers is a promising oil spill cleanup technique in wetland environments.

# CHAPTER 4

## A COMPARISON OF BIOSTIMULATION AND PHYTOREMEDIATION OF CRUDE OIL IN WETLAND MESOCOSMS

by Qianxin Lin, Irving A. Mendelssohn, Charles B. Henry, Jr., Scott Miles, Edward B. Overton, Ralph J. Portier, and Maud M. Walsh

Biostimulation attempts to accelerate the natural degradation process of contaminants, such as petroleum hydrocarbons, by adding non-bacterial agents to overcome factors that limit bacterial hydrocarbon degradation. The most common biostimulants, shown to enhance oil degradation, are inorganic nutrients (Mikesell et al. 1991; Altas 1993; Bragg et al. 1993; Prince et al. 1993; Venosa et al. 1992, 1996; Lin et al. 1999b). Previous studies (Scherrer and Mille 1990; Lindstrom et al. 1991; McKee and Mendelssohn 1995; Venosa et al. 1996; Wright et al. 1997; Lin and Mendelssohn 1998b; Lin et al. 1999c) indicated that fertilization with inorganic nitrogen and phosphorus enhanced degradation of petroleum hydrocarbons. In a wetland mesocosm experiment, addition of phosphorus and nitrogen significantly increased oil degradation, but nitrogen alone did not (Wright et al. 1997), suggesting that phosphorus may limit microbial degradation of oil in some wetlands. However, biostimulation effectiveness on an oiled shoreline associated with the Exxon Valdez oil spill (Bragg et al. 1993) was determined to depend primarily on the amount of nitrogen fertilizer delivered to the substrate. Thus, the role of N versus P in oil bioremediation has not been clarified.

Phytoremediation, the use of vegetation for the *in-situ* treatment of contaminated soil and sediment, is an emerging technology that promises effective and inexpensive cleanup of pollutants (Stomp et al. 1993; Schnoor et al. 1995). Phytoremediation applies to all plant-influenced biological, chemical, and physical processes that aid in the remediation of contaminants (Cunningham and Breti 1993), such as petroleum hydrocarbons. Phytoremediation has already been shown to have potential for the cleanup of both inorganic pollutants, such as heavy metals, and organic pollutants, including polycyclic aromatic hydrocarbons (PAHs) (Anderson and Walton 1992; Bell 1992; Brown et al. 1995; Salt et al. 1995; Reilley et al. 1996; Kling 1997; Lin and Mendelssohn 1997, 1998a and 1998b; Lin et al. 1999b; Banks et al. 1999; Liste and Alexander 2000b). However, few studies have focused on the efficacy of phytoremediation for oil spill cleanup in wetland environments. In addition, most biostimulation studies in wetland environments have assumed that the primary effect of fertilization is the direct stimulation of bacterial activity. However, the fertilization may accelerate oil degradation through plant-associated processes, e.g., uptake or plant-stimulated microbial activity. The importance of the vegetation, per se, in the remediation of wetlands with fertilizers has not been investigated.

The objectives of this study were to (a) determine the effectiveness of biostimulation with inorganic nitrogen and phosphorus, singly and in combination, on oil degradation and (b) separate the effect of phytoremediation from biostimulation in accelerating oil degradation.

## Materials and Methods

### Experimental Design

In the greenhouse, the following treatments were randomly applied and their effects on oil biodegradation determined: (1) phytoremediation with *Spartina alterniflora* or no plants, (2) nitrogen fertilization, and (3) phosphorus fertilization. The experimental design was a completely randomized block with a 2 x 3 x 2 factorial treatment arrangement. We compared phytoremediation by *S. alterniflora* with the soil without plants. We also evaluated the effect of biostimulation of oil at three nitrogen dosage rates (high = 466 kg N/ha;, low = 233 kg N/ha; and 0 kg N/ha nitrogen fertilizer) on oil degradation. In addition, we compared the biostimulation effect of nitrogen fertilizer with that of phosphorus fertilization (175 and 0 kg P/ha). Treatment-level combinations were replicated five times. A total of 60 experimental units were used in this experiment.

**Experimental Procedures**

Artificially weathered (25% by volume) south Louisiana crude oil was applied at a level of 2 L/m$^2$ to a mixture of two potting soils (50% by volume of Jiffy Mix, Jiffy Products of America, Chicago, IL and 50% of VitaHume potting soil, Hyponex Corporation, Marysville, OH). This oil dosage is equivalent to about 20 mg oil/g dry soil. The soil and the applied oil were well mixed, then placed into individual 8-liter buckets. Directly mixing the oil with the soil was done to reduce the variation in the initial oil concentrations among experimental units, a common condition when oil is added to the soil surface (Chapters 2 and 3). Fifteen (15) culms (shoots and intact roots and rhizomes) of *Spartina alterniflora*, free of soil surrounding the roots, were transplanted into each bucket. The experiment was conducted in the greenhouse. High (133 kg N/ha) and low (67 kg N/ha) rates of soluble nitrogen fertilizer (NH$_4$Cl) and soluble phosphorus fertilizer (50 kg P/ha of NaH$_2$PO$_4$) were dissolved in water and applied to the soil surface of the appropriate fertilization experimental units 1, 8, and 16 weeks after transplanting *S. alterniflora*. Half of the previous amounts of N and P were applied to the appropriate experimental units after 20 weeks to ensure reasonable concentrations of inorganic nutrients in the final four weeks of the experiment. The four fertilizer applications resulted in a total of 466 kg N/ha and 233 kg N/ha for the high and low nitrogen treatments, respectively, and 175 kg P/ha for the phosphorus application treatment. The water levels in each experimental unit were kept at 0.5 cm above the soil surface by daily watering the pots with tap water.

At the termination of the six-month experiment, the mesocosms were sampled for (1) petroleum hydrocarbon chemistry, such as total targeted aromatic hydrocarbons (TTAH) and total targeted normal hydrocarbons (TTNH) to identify and quantify the degree of oil biodegradation; (2) soil microbial responses, such as oil-degrading microbes and microbial respiration rates to determine the effect of the bioremediation products on the microbial communities that are performing the oil biodegradation; (3) soil chemistry to determine the effect of the bioremediation products on those factors that limit the growth of microbes and plants; and, (4) plant response, such as plant photosynthetic rate, plant stem density, and plant biomass to evaluate the effects of fertilizer on plant growth and its relationship to oil degradation.

Statistical analysis was conducted with the SAS system (SAS 1990). General Linear Model (GLM) was used to test for statistically significant differences ($P<0.05$) among the treatments and Duncan's multiple range test was used to determine significant differences among the main factors. Treatment-level combination differences, if interactions of main factors were significant, were tested with least square means.

**Methods**

Plant Response

*Photosynthetic Rate.* Leaf photosynthetic rate was measured to indicate plant growth status. A portable photosynthesis system, including an infrared gas analyzer (IRGA) (The Analytical Developmemt Co. Ltd, (ADC) model LCA-2), an ADC air flow control unit, and an ADC Parkinson leaf chamber, was used. Sample air, taken 5 m aboveground to obtain relatively stable CO$_2$ concentrations, was led through the ADC air flow control unit at the flow rate of 5 ml/s during photosynthetic rate measurements. Measurements were conducted at a quantum flux density of 2000 µmol/m$^2$/s provided by a Kodak projector lamp. An intact, attached and fully expanded young leaf was enclosed in the leaf chamber and the difference in CO$_2$ concentration and humidity between inlet and outlet air was measured. Photosynthetic rate (CO$_2$ exchange) was calculated in accordance with von Caemmerer and Farquhar (1981) and expressed as µmol CO$_2$/m$^2$/s

*Plant Stem Density.* Plant stem density was measured by direct counting of stem number in each experimental unit and expressed as the number of stems per pot.

*Average and Maximum Shoot Height.* Canopy height of the transplants was measured to the nearest centimeter.

*Aboveground Biomass.* Plant aboveground biomass of *S. alterniflora* was analyzed at the end of a six-month experimental period to determine the treatment effect on plant growth. Plant aboveground material was clipped at the soil surface, dried in an oven at 65°C to constant weight, and weighed.

*Belowground Biomass of the Transplant.* Plant belowground biomass of *S. alterniflora* was determined by washing all soil from the belowground plant material at the end of the experiment, dring in an oven at 65°C to constant weight, and weighing.

*Water Evapo-Transpirational Rate.* Evapo-transpirational water losses, the combination of water loss by transpiration from plant leaves and by evaporation from the water surface, were determined by measuring the mass water loss from the each experimental unit in a 24-hour period. First, the water table in the container was raised to 0.5 cm above the soil surface and the experimental unit weighed. After 24 hours, the mass of the experiment unit was again determined. The difference in mass over a 24-hour period was defined as the evapo-transpirational water loss.

Soil Response

*Soil Respiration Rate.* *In-situ* measurements of soil respiration rate, an indicator of soil microbial activity, were made with an infra-red gas analyzer (IRGA) by measuring carbon dioxide production from soil. A PVC chamber (4 cm in diameter and 8 cm in height) with one open end was equipped with an inlet and an outlet for air flow through the chamber. The open end of the chamber was inserted into the soil 4 cm below the soil surface. The air flow rate through the chamber was held constant at 300 ml per minute by an ADC mass flow controller. The respiratory $CO_2$ produced from the soil resulted in a difference in $CO_2$ concentration between inlet and outlet that was measured by an ADC infra-red gas analyzer. Soil respiration was calculated based on the $CO_2$ exchange rate from the soil per unit surface area.

*Soil Redox Potential.* Soil redox potentials at 3 and 12 cm depths were determined with bright platinum electrodes and a calomel reference electrode. Readings were taken with a portable pH/mV digital meter. The potential of a calomel reference electrode (+244 mV) was added to each value to calculate Eh (Patrick et al. 1996).

*Soil Nutrient Concentrations.* Interstitial water samples were withdrawn from soil sods with a simple apparatus as described by McKee et al. (1988). This consisted of a small diameter (3 mm inside diameter) rigid plastic tube, containing numerous ca. 0.5 mm diameter holes covered with 3 to 4 layers of cheesecloth, connected to a 30 ml syringe. The collected interstitial water was filtered through a 0.45 μm syringe filter. Inorganic nutrients in the filtered interstitial water were analyzed to determine the effect of product application on soil fertility and other variables. Ammonium-nitrogen ($NH_4$) and nitrate-nitrogen ($NO_3 + NO_2$) were analyzed with an auto-analyzer. Total inorganic nitrogen was determined as the sum of $NH_4$, $NO_3$, and $NO_2$-nitrogen concentrations. Phosphate was measured by the Murphy-Riley procedure (Parsons et al. 1984).

*Oil-Degrading Microbes.* Petroleum-utilizing populations were determined at the end of a six-month experimental period. Soil samples were collected from 0 to 8 cm below the soil surface at the termination of the experiment. Oil-degrading population were tracked using plate count methods. A minimal salts agar to which 50 ppm naphthalene and 50 ppm cresol were added as the sole carbon source was used for the selective culturing of petroleum-degrading organisms. All microbial population measurements were reported per gram dry weight gram.

*Residual Oil Chemistry in the Soil.* Total targeted normal hydrocarbons (TTNH) and total targeted aromatic hydrocarbons (TTAH) were analyzed to determine the oil degradation rates. . Soil samples were collected from the soil surface to the bottom (about 16 cm below the soil surface) at the termination of the experiment from each experimental unit, thoroughly homogenized, and extracted using a modified EPA method 3550. Approximately 20 grams of wet soil were extracted using dichloromethane and sodium sulfate as a chemical drying agent (Venosa et al. 1996; Sauer and Boehm 1991; Henry and Overton 1993; Henry et al. 1993), then reduced to a final volume of 10 ml. A field treatment composite was then analyzed by gas chromatography-mass spectrometry (GC/MS) operated in the Selective Ion Monitoring (SIM) Mode to characterize compositional changes in targeted normal hydrocarbons (NH) and aromatic hydrocarbons (AH). Although these targeted AH generally represent less than 5% of the bulk oil composition, they are essential to characterize petroleum source, identify potential biological effects, determine exposure pathways, and monitor weathering trends and degradation of the oil (Sauer and Boehm 1991; Roques et al. 1994). The targeted aromatic hydrocarbons are listed in Table 1 (Chapter 1).

**Results**

<u>Responses of *S. alterniflora* to the Treatments</u>

The effects of biostimulants on *Spartina alterniflora*, the dominant plant in Atlantic and Gulf coast salt marshes of the United States, were estimated by measuring photosynthetic rate, stem density, plant shoot height, and above- and belowground biomass. Nitrogen application significantly increased photosynthetic rate (Fig. 44), plant stem density (Fig. 45), and plant shoot height (Fig. 46) of *S. alterniflora*. They were significantly higher in the treatments with a low dosage of nitrogen than without nitrogen application, and significantly higher in the treatments with a high dosage of nitrogen than the low dosage (Fig. 44 to 463). Phosphorus application increased photosynthetic rate (Fig. 44), plant stem density (Fig. 45), and plant shoot height (Fig. 46) of *S. alterniflora* in addition to nitrogen.

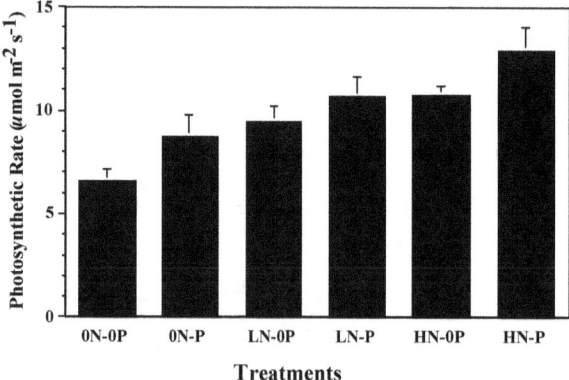

Figure 44. Effect of nitrogen and phosphorus application on photosynthetic rate of *Spartina alterniflora* six months after the treatments. Values are means (n=5) with standard errors. 0N: no nitrogen application, 0P: no phosphorus application, P: 175 kg P/ha, LN: 233 kg N/ha, HN: 466 kg N/ha.

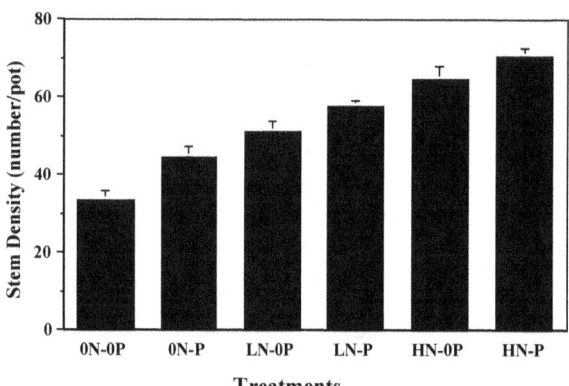

Figure 45. Effect of nitrogen and phosphorus application on stem density of *Spartina alterniflora* six months after the treatments. Values are means (n=5) with standard errors. 0N: no nitrogen application, 0P: no phosphorus application, P: 175 kg P/ha, LN: 233 kg N/ha, HN: 466 kg N/ha.

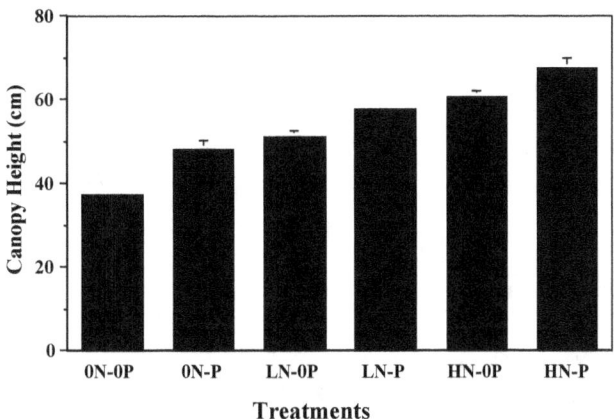

Figure 46. Effect of nitrogen and phosphorus application on canopy height of *Spartina alterniflora* six months after the treatments. Values are means (n=5) with standard errors. 0N: no nitrogen application, 0P: no phosphorus application, P: 175 kg P/ha, LN: 233 kg N/ha, HN: 466 kg N/ha.

Both nitrogen and phosphorus applications significantly increased aboveground and belowground biomass of *S. alterniflora*. At the termination of the experiment 6 months after the treatment, aboveground and belowground biomass of *S. alterniflora* were significantly higher in the treatment with a low dosage of nitrogen than without nitrogen application. Also, aboveground and belowground biomass of *S alterniflora* were significantly higher in the treatment with a high dosage of nitrogen than the low dosage (Figs. 47 and 48, Table 13). In addition, phosphorus application significantly increased aboveground and belowground biomass of *S. alterniflora* compared to the treatments without phosphorus application.

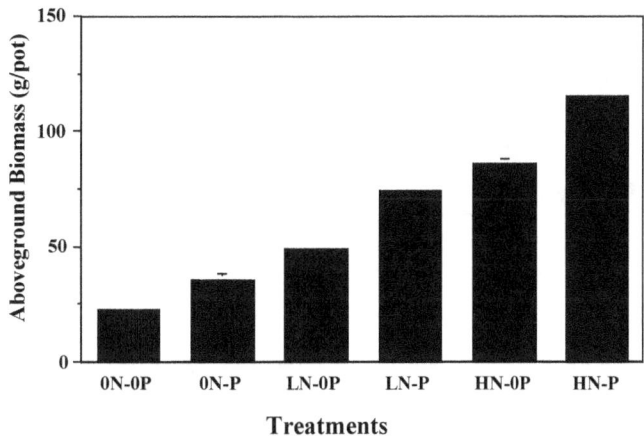

Figure 47. Effect of nitrogen and phosphorus application on aboveground biomass of *Spartina alterniflora* six months after the treatments. Values are means (n=5) with standard errors. 0N: no nitrogen application, 0P: no phosphorus application, P: 175 kg P/ha, LN: 233 kg N/ha, HN: 466 kg N/ha.

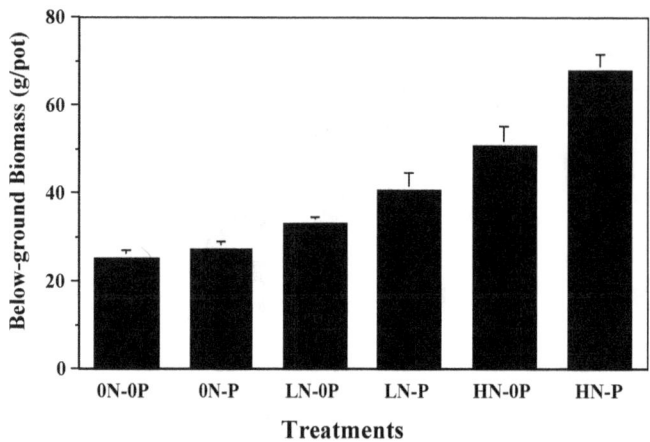

Figure 48. Effect of nitrogen and phosphorus application on belowground biomass of *Spartina alterniflora* six months after the treatments. Values are means (n=5) with standard errors. 0N: no nitrogen application, 0P: no phosphorus application, P: 175 kg P/ha, LN: 233 kg N/ha, HN: 466 kg N/ha.

Table 13.  Statistical Table for the Transplant Variables with P-Values Provided for Main Factors and Their Interactions

| Plant Variables | N | P | N*P |
|---|---|---|---|
| Photosynthetic rate | 0.0001 | 0.0114 | 0.8135 |
| Stem density | 0.0001 | 0.0007 | 0.5338 |
| Canopy height | 0.0001 | 0.0001 | 0.2179 |
| Aboveground Biomass | 0.0001 | 0.0001 | 0.0003 |
| Belowground Biomass | 0.0001 | 0.0015 | 0.0741 |

N: nitrogen application; P: phosphorus application;
N*P: interaction of nitrogen and phosphorus applications.

Plant evapo-transpiration rate was measured to determine the effect of the transplants and fertilizer application on water loss rate from the experimental units.  Evapo-transpiration rates in the treatments with phytoremediation by *S. alterniflora* were significantly higher than in those without transplants (Fig. 49, Table 14). Water evapo-transpiration rates in the treatments receiving nitrogen and phosphorus fertilizer were significantly higher than treatment without fertilizer (Fig. 49, Table 14).  A significant interaction between phytoremediation and nitrogen fertilizer application (Table 14) indicated that the higher evapo-transpiration rate in the treatments with nitrogen occurred only in the presence of transplants.

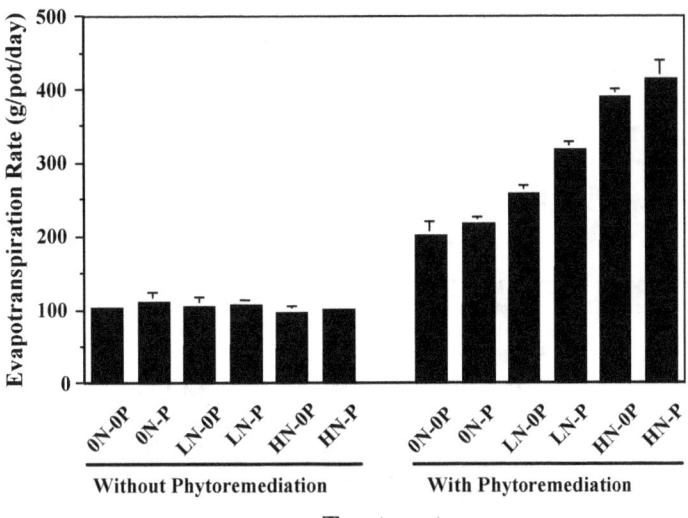

Figure 49. Effect of phytoremediation and nitrogen and phosphorus application on evapo-transpiration rate six months after the treatments. Values are means (n=5) with standard errors. 0N: no nitrogen application, 0P: no phosphorus application, P: 175 kg P/ha, LN: 233 kg N/ha, HN: 466 kg N/ha.

Table 14. Statistical Table for the Soil Variables and Residual Oil Concentration with P-Values Provided for Main Factors and Their Interactions

| Parameter | Main Factors | | | Interaction | | | |
|---|---|---|---|---|---|---|---|
| | Phyto | N | P | Phyto*N | Phyto*P* | N*P | Phyto* N*P |
| EH 3cm | 0.0001 | 0.2291 | 0.6799 | 0.3920 | 0.3133 | 0.7384 | 0.5100 |
| EH 12cm | 0.0266 | 0.4366 | 0.4571 | 0.7476 | 0.1439 | 0.7873 | 0.3173 |
| Evapo-transpiration | 0.0001 | 0.0001 | 0.0073 | 0.0001 | 0.0628 | 0.5042 | 0.2831 |
| Soil Respiration | 0.5471 | 0.6594 | 0.7499 | 0.6611 | 0.8600 | 0.8239 | 0.9629 |
| Interstitial Inorganic Nitrogen | 0.0198 | 0.0344 | 0.2928 | 0.0297 | 0.3125 | 0.2256 | 0.2325 |
| Interstitial Phosphate | 0.0002 | 0.3603 | 0.8841 | 0.1597 | 0.4555 | 0.5933 | 0.3528 |
| TTNH | 0.0001 | 0.7023 | 0.1853 | 0.8279 | 0.4521 | 0.4927 | 0.1533 |
| TTAH | 0.0146 | 0.0608 | 0.6141 | 0.0010 | 0.8791 | 0.9966 | 0.6107 |

Phyto: phytoremediation treatment; N: nitrogen application; P: phosphorus application; N*P: interaction of nitrogen and phosphorus applications, etc.

Responses of Soil Variables

Soil parameters (e.g., soil Eh and nutrients) were measured to determine if addition of the fertilizer and transplants had any effect on the soil environment. Soil redox potential is a measure of the degree to which a soil is oxidized or reduced. Higher redox potentials signify more aerated soils. Soil redox potential was significantly higher in the treatments receiving transplants than those without transplants for both 3 and 12 cm below the soil surface (Figs. 50 and 51), indicating that transplants aerated the soil by transporting atmospheric air to their rhizosphere. For example, average redox potential at the 3 cm soil depth was +168 mV (± 16 standard error, n=30) for the treatment receiving *S. alterniflora* and -54 mV (± 15 standard error, n=30) for the treatment without transplants (Fig 50). Average redox potential at the 12 cm soil depth was +12 mV (± 18 standard error, n=30) for the treatment receiving *S. alterniflora* and -46 (± 17 standard error, n=30) mV for the treatment without transplants (Fig 51). The addition of nitrogen and phosphorus did not significantly affect soil redox potential at 3 and 12 cm depth.

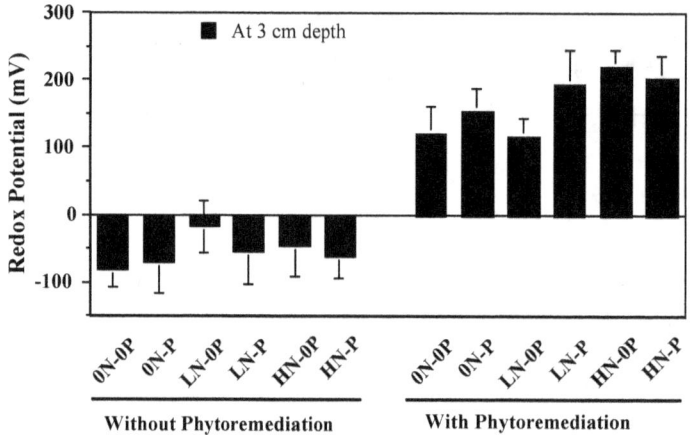

Figure 50. Effect of phytoremediation and nitrogen and phosphorus application on soil redox potential at 3 cm below the soil surface six months after the treatments. Values are means (n=5) with standard errors. 0N: no nitrogen application, 0P: no phosphorus application, P: 175 kg P/ha, LN: 233 kg N/ha, HN: 466 kg N/ha.

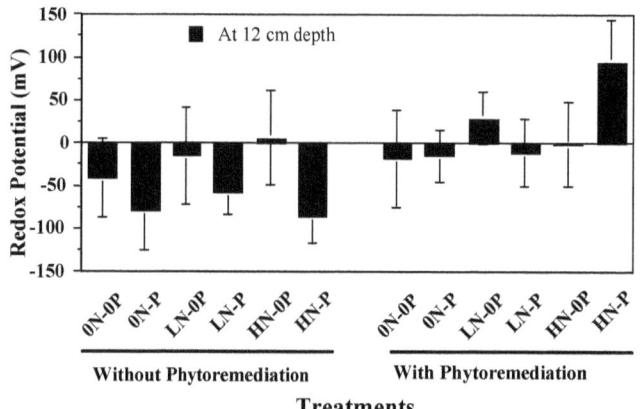

Figure 51. Effect of phytoremediation and nitrogen and phosphorus application on soil redox potential at 12 cm below the soil surface six months after the treatments. Values are means (n=5) with standard errors. 0N: no nitrogen application, 0P: no phosphorus application, P: 175 kg P/ha, LN: 233 kg N/ha, HN: 466 kg N/ha.

Interstitial inorganic nitrogen and phosphorus were analyzed to determine the available nutrient status of the experimental units and their effect on phytoremediation. Phytoremediation by *S. alterniflora* and nitrogen addition significantly affected interstitial inorganic nitrogen concentration (Fig. 52). A significant interaction between phytoremediation and nitrogen fertilizer application showed that the higher interstitial nitrogen in the treatments receiving nitrogen fertilizer occurred only in the absence of phytoremediation by *S. alterniflora*. In the presence of the plants, plant uptake of nitrogen may control the interstitial nitrogen concentration. Phosphorus addition did not affect interstitial inorganic nitrogen. Furthermore, phytoremediation by *S. alterniflora* significantly affected interstitial phosphate concentration (Fig. 53). Average interstitial phosphate concentration was significantly higher in the treatments without plants than those with plants, with 9.66 mg/L in the former versus 7.45 mg/L in the latter six months after treatment initiation (Figs. 50B). However, the addition of nitrogen and phosphorus fertilizer did not affect interstitial phosphorus concentrations compared to the treatments without fertilization.

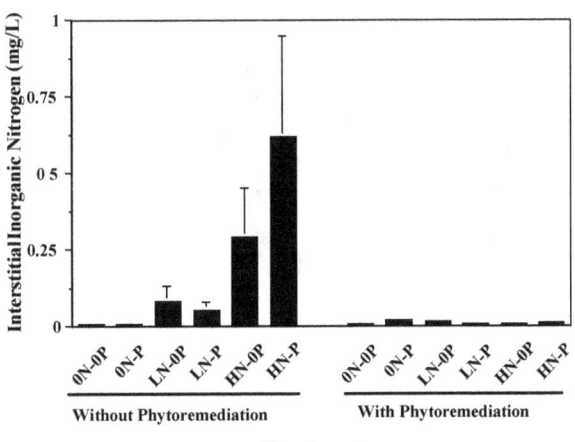

Figure 52. Effect of phytoremediation and nitrogen and phosphorus application on interstitial inorganic nitrogen six months after the treatments. Values are means (n=5) with standard errors. 0N: no nitrogen application, 0P: no phosphorus application, P: 175 kg P/ha, LN: 233 kg N/ha, HN: 466 kg N/ha.

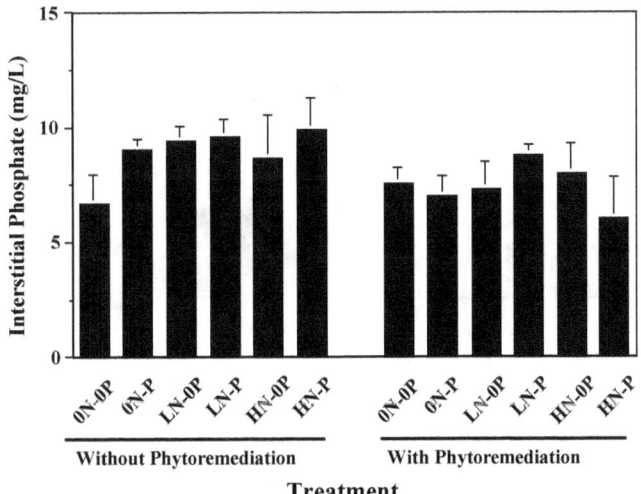

Figure 53. Effect of phytoremediation and nitrogen and phosphorus application on interstitial phosphate concentration six months after the treatments. Values are means (n=5) with standard errors. 0N: no nitrogen application, 0P: no phosphorus application, P: 175 kg P/ha, LN: 233 kg N/ha, HN: 466 kg N/ha.

Microbial soil respiration and oil-degrading microbial populations were measured to determine the treatment effects and their relationship to oil degradation. Generally, neither phytoremediation by *S. alterniflora* nor addition of nitrogen and phosphorus fertilizer significantly affected microbial soil respiration rate (Fig. 54) and oil-degrading microbial populations (Fig. 55). A large variation was observed for these two variables.

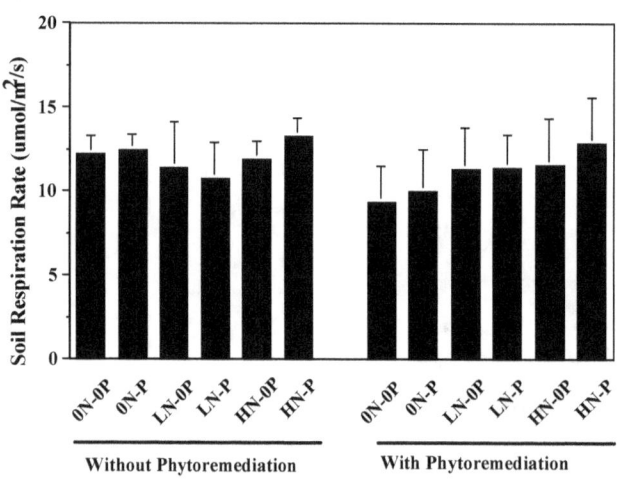

Figure 54. Effect of phytoremediation and nitrogen and phosphorus application on soil respiration rate six months after the treatments. Values are means (n=5) with standard errors. 0N: no nitrogen application, 0P: no phosphorus application, P: 175 kg P/ha, LN: 233 kg N/ha, HN: 466 kg N/ha.

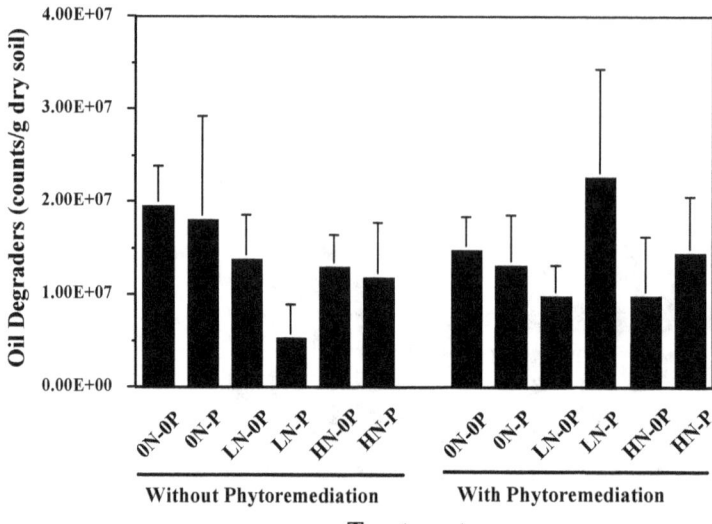

Figure 55. Effect of phytoremediation and nitrogen and phosphorus application on oil-degrading microbial populations six months after the treatments. Values are means (n=5) with standard errors. 0N: no nitrogen application, 0P: no phosphorus application, P: 175 kg P/ha, LN: 233 kg N/ha, HN: 466 kg N/ha

**Oil Chemistry**

<u>Alkane Degradation</u>

Phytoremediation by *S. alterniflora* enhanced alkane degradation in the present study. The concentration of residual total targeted normal hydrocarbons (TTNH) was significantly lower (p<0.0001) in the treatments with *S. alterniflora* than in those without *S. alterniflora*, with 4597 µg/g dry soil (± 241 standard error, n=30) in the former versus 10124 µg/g (± 979 standard error, n=30) after six months of treatment (Fig. 56). However, addition of nitrogen and phosphorus did not significantly affect concentrations of residual total targeted normal hydrocarbons.

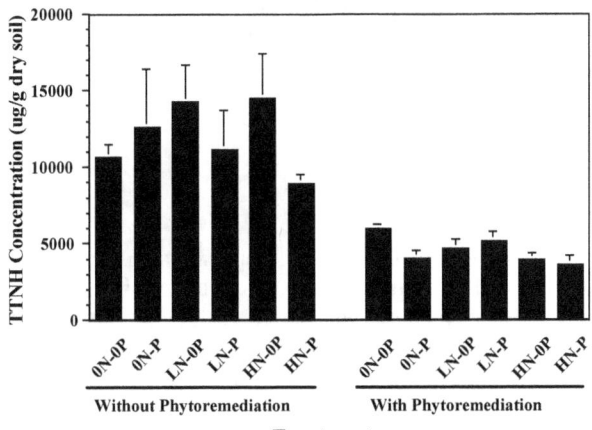

Figure 56. Effect of phytoremediation and nitrogen and phosphorus application on total targeted normal hydrocarbons (TTNH) six months after the treatments. Values are means (n=5) with standard errors. 0N: no nitrogen application, 0P: no phosphorus application, P: 175 kg P/ha, LN: 233 kg N/ha, HN: 466 kg N/ha.

<u>Aromatic Hydrocarbon Degradation</u>

Phytoremediation by *S. alterniflora* enhanced aromatic hydrocarbon degradation. Concentrations of residual total targeted aromatic hydrocarbons (TTAH) were significantly lower in the treatments with *S. alterniflora* than in those without *S. alterniflora*, with 43.4 µg/g dry soil (± 3.7 standard error, n=30) in the former versus 55.7 µg/g (± 3.8 standard error, n=30) after six months of treatment (Figs. 57, Table 14). Application of nitrogen fertilizer tended to decrease (p=0.0608) the concentration of residual total targeted aromatic hydrocarbons compared to those without nitrogen application. A significant interaction (p<0.001) between phytoremediation and nitrogen fertilizer application demonstrated that nitrogen only had a significant effect in decreasing residual total targeted aromatic hydrocarbons when plants were present. For example, the concentration of residual total targeted aromatic hydrocarbons was 22.6 µg/g dry soil (± 2.7 standard error, n=10) in the treatment receiving high nitrogen dosage (with and without applying phosphorus) combined with *S. alterniflora*, compared to 61.8 µg/g dry soil (± 10.4 standard error, n=10) in the treatment receiving high nitrogen dosage (with and without applying phosphorus) but without *S. alterniflora*. However, the addition of phosphorus alone did not significantly affect the concentration of residual total targeted aromatic hydrocarbons.

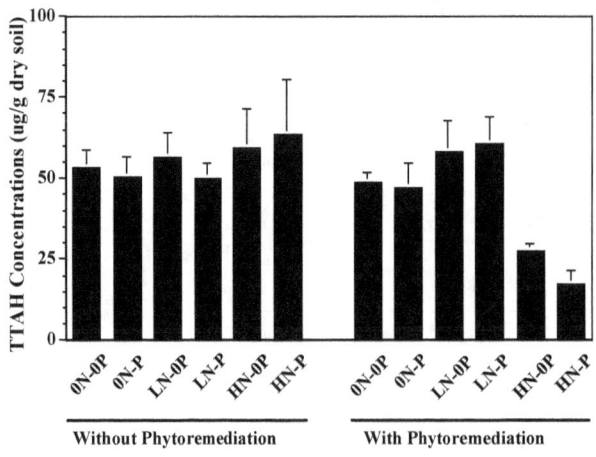

**Figure 57.** Effect of phytoremediation and nitrogen and phosphorus application on total targeted aromatic hydrocarbons (TTNH) six months after the treatments. Values are means (n=5) with standard errors. 0N: no nitrogen application, 0P: no phosphorus application, P: 175 kg P/ha, LN: 233 kg N/ha, HN: 466 kg N/ha.

**Discussion**

In the present study, both nitrogen and phosphorus application significantly enhanced plant growth. Phytoremediation by the salt marsh plant *S. alterniflora* significantly increased soil redox potential, indicating a more oxidized soil environment that may enhance aerobic oil degradation. More importantly, concentrations of residual alkane and aromatic hydrocarbons were significantly lower in the treatments receiving phytoremediation, especially when combined with phosphorus and the high nitrogen dosage.

Phytoremediation by *S. alterniflora* enhanced oil degradation, with a significant lower concentration of total targeted normal hydrocarbons (TTNH) and total targeted aromatic hydrocarbons (TTAH) in the treatments with phytoremediation compared to those without phytoremediation. A number of studies have found phytoremediation enhancement of hydrocarbon degradation. Liste and Alexander (2000b) reported that more pyrene was degraded in the presence of roots of all nine plant species tested than in un-planted soil. Within approximately 8 weeks, as much as 74% of the pyrene disappeared from vegetated soil compared to 40% or less from unplanted soil. Phytoremediation by *Typha latifolia* reduced 90% of the hydrocarbons in a artificial wetland over a 360-day period (Salmon et al. 1998). Banks et al. (1999) reported that the presence of plants of *Festuca arandinacea* enhanced the degradation of highly adsorbed, recalcitrant benzo(a)pyrene in soils in a greenhouse experiment. Guenther et al. (1996) reported that in a rhizosphere sod system with growing ryegrass in the laboratory, aliphatic hydrocarbons disappeared faster than in unvegetated columns. These results indicate that biodegradation of hydrocarbons in the rhizosphere is stimulated by plant roots. The present study supported these findings, and again suggested the promise and potential of phytoremediation of oil.

Higher plants are being used to enhance the remediation of soils contaminated with recalcitrant organic compounds, such as petroleum hydrocarbons in oil spills. Several possible mechanisms of enhanced oil degradation via phytoremediation have been cited although mechanisms of action are poorly understood. The soil physico-chemical environment can effect soil microbial activity and plant condition, thus affecting microbial degradation rate. Oxygen is an important electron acceptor for microbial oil degradation (Mikesell *et al.* 1991; Lee and Swindoll 1993; Hurst et al. 1996; Wilson et al. 1999). Oil degradation rate is generally much slower in a water saturated anaerobic condition than an aerobic environment (Hambrick et al. 1980, Lin and Mendelssohn 1998a). Hurst et al. (1996) reported that 45% and 55% of pyrene and PAH compounds were degraded under soil gas oxygen concentrations between 2% and 21%. No statistically significant mineralization was found to occur at 0% oxygen. In a laboratory bioremediation study of hydrocarbon contaminated groundwater and sediment, Wilson et al. (1999) found that only toluene was degraded at initial oxygen levels ranging from 0 to 1 mg $O_2$/L. Naphthalene degradation was observed in addition to toluene removal at initial oxygen levels ranging from 1.5 to 2.0 mg $O_2$/L. This range represents a threshold level below which naphthalene could not be degraded under the experimental conditions. At oxygen levels greater than or equal to 7 mg $O_2$/L, some removal of all aromatic compounds was observed. It is well known that many wetland plants can transport oxygen from the atmosphere through plant air-space tissue to aerate the soil rhizosphere (Armstrong 1978; Smirnoff and Crawford 1983; Teal and Kanwisher 1966). In the present study, phytoremediation by *S. alterniflora* significantly increased soil redox potential, indicating a more oxidized soil environment in the treatments receiving transplants. Therefore, increased oxygen supply in the rhizosphere likely increased aerobic oil degradation in the treatments with phytoremediation.

Another possible mechanism of action in the phytoremediation process is adsorption of the organic contaminant onto the surface of the roots and subsequent uptake and/or degradation, thus reducing its concentration in the soil. By comparing affinity and adsorption of plant roots for naphthalene, a polycyclic aromatic hydrocarbon, for tall fescue and alfalfa, Schwab et al. (1998) found that alfalfa roots had approximately twice the affinity for naphthalene than fescue roots and concluded that lipid content is a controlling factor in adsorption of naphthalene onto plant roots. In a study determining PAH concentrations in the rhizosphere of plants grown in soil containing phenanthrene or pyrene, Liste and Alexander (2000a) reported that the rhizosphere of several plant species temporarily contained appreciably more phenanthrene and pyrene than unplanted soil, but those PAHs were degraded with time, suggesting that plants accumulate such hydrophobic compounds in the rhizosphere after facilitating their transport toward the roots. Lytle and Lytle (1987) reported that *Juncus roemerianus* uptakes petroleum hydrocarbons from marsh sediments, thus reducing oil concentration. Burken and Schnoor (1998) reported that translocation and subsequent transpiration of volatile organic compounds from the leaves to the atmosphere was shown to be a significant pathway of hydrocarbon loss. In the present study, phytoremediation with *S. alterniflora* had up to a seven-fold higher transpirational water loss from the plant leaf surface. The transpiration stream of *S. alterniflora* would have likely facilitated the hydrocarbon transport toward the roots, uptake by the plants, metabolism in the plants, and/or transpiration of volatile hydrocarbons to the atmosphere, thus reducing the concentration of TTNH and TTAH in the soil.

Many studies have indicated that bioremediation with fertilizers, such as nitrogen and phosphorus, increases oil degradation. Swannell et al. (1999) reported that bioremediation of a mixture of Forties Crude Oil and Heavy Fuel Oil stranded on shorelines of Bullwell Bay, Milford Haven, UK, after the grounding of the Sea Empress in 1996. Both a weekly application of mineral nutrients dissolved in seawater and a single application of a slow-release fertilizer supplied the proportional amount of nitrogen and phosphorus enhanced oil degradation. In a mesocosm experiment, addition of phosphorus and nitrogen significantly increased oil degradation, but nitrogen alone did not (Wright et al. 1997). In a laboratory study on the effects of nitrogen and phosphorus levels on petroleum bioremediation, Walworth and Reynolds, (1995) reported that at 10° C, degradation rates of diesel fuel were not affected by fertility treatments. At 20° C, the rates were increased by the addition of P, but unaffected by N. These results suggest that phosphorus may limit microbial degradation of oil in some cases. However, in an experiment associated with the Exxon Valdez oil spill (Bragg et al. 1993), effectiveness was determined to depend primarily on the amount of nitrogen fertilizer delivered to the sediment. In a laboratory bioremediation study of crude oil, Chang et al. (1996) reported that at 3% oil in the soil, addition of P, without N, generally did not enhance biodegradation. Addition of N, without P, approximately tripled the quantity of oil degraded. Addition of P and N together did not increase biodegradation of oil more than the addition of N alone, suggesting the importance of N in bioremediation of oil. At 6 and 9% oil concentrations, $CO_2$ evolution increased by adding P and N together in comparison to adding N alone, and total petroleum hydrocarbon (TPH) biodegradation increased by 30% in 60 days. These results suggest that nitrogen may be more important in microbial degradation of oil than phosphorus, but phosphorus can increase oil degradation once nitrogen limitations are relieved.

In the present study, in the absence of the marsh plant of *S. alterniflora*, application of nitrogen and phosphorus, singly or in combination, did not affect soil oil-degrading microbial populations, soil respiration, and residual concentrations of TTNH and TTAH. High concentrations of the background phosphorus level mute the effect of the added P on oil degradation in the current study. Interstitial phosphorus concentration was fairly high, with more than 7 ppm in the control treatment even after 6 months. Thus, addition of phosphorus did not increase interstitial phosphate concentration. Also, the addition of nitrogen, when transplants were absent, did not affect the residual TTNH and TTAH, although interstitial nitrogen concentration increased. This suggests that, in the absence of plants, the role of N and P fertilization in oil degradation may be limited, especially in water-saturated soils. In the presence of the marsh plant of *S. alterniflora*, high nitrogen, with or without phosphorus, significantly decreased TTAH by more than 2 fold. Nitrogen and phosphorus addition significantly increased plant growth with higher photosynthetic rate, stem density, and above- and belowground biomass. Increased plant growth was responsible for the increased evapo-transpiration rate and soil redox potential. Thus, fertilizer-increased plant growth enhanced the degradation of the oil due possibly to higher aerobic oil degradation, plant uptake, metabolism in the plants, and transpiration of volatile hydrocarbons to the atmosphere. These results suggest that the effectiveness of fertilization on oil degradation may be dependent on phytoremediation with fertilizer-enhanced plants.

The effect of fertilizer on oil degradation was also related to phytoremediation in several other studies (Reynolds et al. 1999; Wright et al. 1997; Lin and Mendelssohn 1997 and 1998). Reynolds et al. (1999) reported that in a 34-week field study, total petroleum hydrocarbon (TPH) concentrations of a diesel-contaminated soil decreased significantly more in the rhizosphere plus nutrient treatment compared to the control that was not vegetated with bahiagrass or fertilized. In a mesocosm system containing *S. alterniflora*, Wright et al. (1997) reported that addition of phosphorus and nitrogen significantly increased oil degradation. Lin and Mendelssohn (1997, 1998a) reported that in the absence of plants, fertilization with nitrogen and phosphorus did not significantly affect residual oil degradation. However, fertilizer significantly enhanced the effect of phytoremediation on oil degradation by plants such as *J. roemerianus*, *S. alterniflora*, and *S. patens*. All these results suggest that fertilization may increase oil degradation through phytoremediation, hence the important of vegetation in accelerating oil degradation.

**Summary**

Both nitrogen and phosphorus application significantly enhanced plant growth. Plant photosynthetic rate, stem density, and above- and belowground biomass of *S. alterniflora* increased with increasing nitrogen dosages. Phosphorus application additionally increased plant growth in each nitrogen application level. Fertilizer-increased plant growth was responsible for increased evapo-transpiration rate and soil redox potential. Phytoremediation by the salt marsh plant *S. alterniflora* significantly increased soil redox potential, indicating a more oxidized soil environment that may enhance aerobic oil degradation. More importantly, concentrations of residual alkanes (TTNH) were significantly lower in the treatment receiving phytoremediation by *S. alterniflora* compared to those without the plants. In addition, concentrations of residual aromatic hydrocarbons (TTAH) were significantly lower in the treatment receiving phytoremediation by *S. alterniflora* compared to those without *S. alterniflora*, and were lowest in the treatment receiving *S. alterniflora* in combination with application of high doses of nitrogen. This result suggests that high levels of nitrogen additionally increase the effect of phytoremediation on TTAH degradation. However, bioremediation by nitrogen and phosphorus addition, singly or in combination, did not significantly reduce residual oil concentration in the absence of *S. alterniflora*. The current study indicates the potential of phytoremediation for the cleanup of hydrocarbon contaminated soil in coastal wetlands. In addition, bioremediation by N and P fertilization enhances the efficacy of oil phytoremediation.

# CHAPTER 5

## PROJECT CONCLUSIONS

Bioremediation by adding non-bacterial agents to enhance natural oil degradation has considerable potential in wetland environments. Efficacy and success of bioremediation of oil to accelerate the biodegradation process depend on the extent of contaminant removal and on the ecological safety of the bioremediation agents. The bioremediation agents used in this research, including a microbial product and inorganic fertilizers, had no negative impacts to the plant, animal, and microbial responses evaluated in this study (Chapter 1). Application of the bioremediation agents at the specified application rates to the salt marsh sods did not adversely affect the marsh macrophyte, *Spartina alterniflora*, various microbial populations and soil respiration, and various infaunal animals including macrofauna and meiofauna. Overall, the bioremediation agents used in this study proved safe to marsh communities.

Application of fertilizer, either in the form of slow release or water soluble, significantly enhanced plant growth with significantly higher photosynthetic rates, stem growth rates, and above- and below-ground biomass of *S. alterniflora* (Chapter 4). In addition, application of fertilizer significantly reduced the concentrations of both the reduced crude oil (Chapter 2) and the artificially weathered crude oil (Chapters 3 and 4). Total targeted normal hydrocarbons (TTNH) and total targeted aromatic hydrocarbons (TTAH), TTNH/hopane and TTAH/hopane, and the $nC-18$/phytane index for evaluation of normal alkane degradation were significantly lower in the treatments with fertilizer compared to those without fertilizer. These results suggest that oil biodegradation in marsh systems may be enhanced by fertilization (biostimulation). Phosphorus application to marsh sods with low interstitial phosphorus significantly increased soil heterotrophic microbial population, oil-degrading microbial populations and soil microbial respiration immediately, and increased TTNH and TTAH degradation, but not in the soils with high initial interstitial phosphorus concentration. The fertilizer-enhanced oil degradation mentioned above occurred only in the presence of the marsh macrophyte, *S. alterniflora*.

The effect of fertilization on oil degradation by directly enhancing soil microbial activity was separated from the phytoremediation effect by comparing bioremediation by added N and P in the absence of plants with that in the presence of *S. alterniflora*. Phytoremediation significantly increased oil degradation. Concentrations of TTNH and TTAH were significantly lower in the treatments receiving *S. alterniflora* than without phytoremediation. In addition, high application rates of nitrogen significantly enhanced the efficacy of phytoremediation on TTAH degradation. In the absence of *S. alterniflora*, however, bioremediation by nitrogen and/or phosphorus addition did not significantly affect residual oil concentration. Thus, the effect of nitrogen on oil degradation in vegetated marshes is most likely through plant-mediated processes. Phosphorus application can be important in stimulating the microbial activity and phytoremediation effect.

Application of the soil oxidant, PermeOx, did not significantly affect oil degradation in the marsh sods. The alkane (TTNH) and aromatic hydrocarbons (TTAH) degradation rates in the treatments receiving the soil oxidant were not significantly higher than the control (Chapter 3). Furthermore, the TTNH and TTAH degradation rates in the treatments receiving the soil oxidant plus fertilizer were not significantly higher than in the treatment receiving fertilizer alone (Chapter 3). These results suggest that there is no positive effect of soil oxidant on oil degradation. Higher degradation rates of alkane (TTNH) and aromatic hydrocarbons (TTAH) in the treatment receiving the soil oxidant plus fertilizer combined with $KH_2PO_4$ (a pH buffer) compared to the fertilizer alone were not due to the soil oxidant, but mainly due to the effect of phosphorus in $KH_2PO_4$ (Chapter 2).

The microbial product did not significantly affect oil degradation. The addition of the microbial product alone and the microbial product with slow release fertilizer did not decrease TTNH and TTAH concentrations in the sediment any more than the control and the slow-release fertilizer, respectively. TTNH/hopane and TTAH/hopane ratios further showed no significant positive effect of microbial product on oil biodegradation. Our results suggest that the presence of microbial hydrocarbon degraders in Louisiana coastal marshes is not limiting oil biodegradation. Thus, this study suggests that the high cost of microbial amendments and soil oxidant application for oil bioremediation may not be warranted in coastal marshes.

Bioremediation with fertilizer enhanced oil degradation in both drained and flooded inundation conditions although oil degradation was greater in drained conditions than in flooded conditions (Chapter 2). In addition, bioremediation with fertilizer enhanced oil degradation in both sandy marsh with low organic matter (<1%) and clay marsh with 19% organic matter. Thus, bioremediation with inorganic nutrient additions has potential for aiding oil spill cleanup efforts in coastal wetlands with various inundation regimes and soil types.

# REFERENCES

Addy, J.M., J.P. Hartley, and P.J.C. Tibbetts. 1984. Ecological effects of low toxicity oil-based mud drilling in the Beatrice Oilfield. Marine Pollution Bulletin 15:429-436.

Alexander, M. 1961. Introduction to Soil Microbiology. New York, John Wiley and Sons, Inc., 472 pp.

Alexander, M. 1989. Biodegradation of Chemicals at Trace Concentrations. Army Research Office, Research Triangle Park, NC. Report No. ARO-23543.19-LS, 28 pp.

Alexander, S.K. and J.W. Webb. 1983. Effects of oil on growth and decomposition of *Spartina alterniflora*. In: Proceedings of 1983 Oil Spill Conference, American Petroleum Institute, Washington, D.C., pp. 529-532.

Alexander, S.K. and J.W. Webb. 1987. Relationship of *Spartina alterniflora* growth to sediment oil content following an oil spill. Proceedings of the 1987 Oil Spill Conference, American Petroleum Institute, Washington, D.C., pp. 445-449.

Amador, J.A. and R.D. Jones. 1993. Nutrient limitations on microbial respiration in peat soils with different total phosphorous content. Soil Biology and Biochemistry 25:793-801.

Anderson, T.A., and B.T. Walton. 1992. Comparative plant uptake and microbial degradation of trichlorethylene in the rhizospheres of five plant species-implications for bioremediation of contaminated surface soils. Oak Ridge, TN: Oak Ridge National Laboratory. Environmental Science Division, Pub. 3809. ORNL/TM-12017; 1992.

Armstrong, W. 1978. Root aeration in the wetland condition. In D.D. Hork and R.M.M. Crawford (ed), Plant Life in Anaerobic Environments. Ann Arbor Science, Ann Arbor, Mich. pp. 169-297.

Arnebrant, K., E. Baath, B. Soderstrom, and H.O. Nohrstedt. 1996. Soil microbial activity in eleven Swedish coniferous forests in relation to site fertility and nitrogen fertilization. Scand. J. Forest Research 11:1-6.

Atlas, R.M. 1993. Bacteria and bioremediation of marine oil spills. Oceanus, 36:2:71-73.

Atlas, R.M. 1995a. Petroleum biodegradation and oil spill bioremediation. Marine Pollution Bulletin 31:178-182.

Atlas, R.M. 1995b. Bioremediation of petroleum pollutants. International Biodeterioration and Biodegradation 35:317-327.

Banks, M.K., E. Lee, and A.P. Schwab. 1999. Evaluation of dissipation mechanisms for benzo(a)pyrene in the rhizosphere of tall fescue. Journal of Environmental Quality. 28(1): 294-298.

Banks, K.M. and A.P. Schwab. 1993. Dissipation of polycyclic aromatic hydrocarbons in the rhizosphere. Symposium on Bioremediation of Hazardous Wastes: Research, Development and Field Evaluations, Washington, DC, Environmental Protection Agency, EPA/600/R-93/054.

Balba, M.T., A.C. Ying, and T.G. McNeice. 1991. Bioremediation of contaminated soil: strategy and case histories. Proceedings of the HMC-South 91: Hazardous Waste, Hazardous Materials/Hazardous Materials Control (HWHM/HMC) Conference, April 24-26, 1991, Houston, TX, pp. 235-241.

Bell, R.M. 1992. Higher plant accumulation of organic pollutants from soils. USEPA, Risk Reduction Engineering Lab. *EPA/600/Sr-92/*138.

Bianchini, M.A., R.J. Portier, *et al.* 1988. Determination of optimal toxicant loading for biological closure of a hazardous waste site. In: Adams, W.J., G.A. Chapman and W. G. Landis (eds.), Aquatic Toxicology and Hazard Assessment: 10th Volume. Philadelphia, American Society for Testing and Materials, pp. 503-516.

Boesch, D.F. and N.N. Rabalais. 1989. Environmental impact of produced water discharges in coastal Louisiana. Rept. to the Louisiana Div. of the Mid-Continent Oil and Gas Assoc. Prepared by the Louisiana Universities Marine Consortium, Chauvin, Louisiana, 287 pp.

Boucher, G. 1980. Impact of Amoco Cadiz oil spill on intertidal and sublittoral meiofauna. Marine Pollution Bulletin 11:95-101.

Braddock, J.F., M.L. Ruth, P.H. Catterall, J.L. Watworth, and K.A. Mccarthy. 1997. Enhancement and Inhibition of microbial activity in hydrocarbon-contaminated arctic soils: implications for nutrient-amended bioremediation. Environmental Science and Technology 31:2078-2084.

Bragg, J.R., R.C. Prince, E.J. Harner, and R.M. Atlas. 1993. Bioremediation effectiveness following the Exxon Valdez spill. Proceedings of the 1993 Oil Spill Conference, American Petroleum Institute, Washington, D.C., pp. 435-447.

Bragg, J.R., R.C. Prince, J.B. Wilkinson, and R.M. Atlas. 1992. Bioremediation for shoreline cleanup following the 1989 Alaska Oil Spill. Exxon Company, USA, Houston, TX. 94 pp.

Brown, S.L., R.L. Chaney, J.S. Angle, and A.J.M. Baker. 1995. Zinc and cadmium uptake by hyperaccumulator Thlaspi caerulescens grown in nutrient solution. Soil SCI. SOC. AM. J., 59:125-133.

Burk, C.J. 1977. A four year analysis of vegetation following an oil spill in a freshwater marsh. Journal of Applied Ecology 14:515-522.

Burken, J.G., and J.L. Schnoor. 1998. Predictive relationships for uptake of organic contaminants by hybrid poplar trees. Environmental-Science-and-Technology. 32 (21) 3379-3385.

Cassidy, M.B., H. Mullineers, H. Lee, and J.T. Trevors. 1997. Mineralization of pentachlorophenol in a contaminated soil by *Pseudomonas sp.* UG30 cells encapsulated in kappa-carrageenan. Journal of Industrial Microbiology and Biotechnology 19:43-48.

Chang, Z.Z., R.W. Weaver, and R.L. Rhykerd. 1996. Oil bioremediation in a high and a low phosphorus soil. Journal of Soil Contamination, 5: 215-224.

Chapelle, F.H. 1999. Bioremediation of petroleum hydrocarbon-contaminated ground water: the perspectives of history and hydrology. Ground Water 37:122-132.

Chianelli, R.R., T. Aczel, R.E. Bare, G.N. George, M.W, Genewithz, M.J. Grossman, C.E. Haith, F.J. Kaiser, R.R. Lessard, R. Liotta, R.L. Mastracchio, V. Minak-Bernero, R.C. Prince, W.K. Robbins, E.I. Stiefel, J.B. Wilkinson, S.M. Hinton, J.R. Bragg, S.J. McMillan, and R.M. Atlas. 1991. Bioremediation technology development and application to the Alaskan spill. Proceedings of the 1991 Oil Spill Conference, American Petroleum Institute, Washington, D.C., pp. 549-558.

Cunningham, S.D. and W.R. Berti. 1993. Remediation of contaminated soil with green plants: an overview. *In Vitro Cellular & Developmental Biology-Plant.* 29p:207-212.

Debusschere, K., S. McMillen, P. Crank, and C. Dash. 1991. The efficiency of bioremediation and geomorphological controls on bioremediation as applied to the Exxon-Valdez spill in Alaska. Unpublished report prepared for Exxon.

DeLaune, R.D., W.H. Patrick, Jr., and R.J. Buresh. 1979. Effect of crude oil on a Louisiana *Spartina alterniflora* salt marsh. Environmental Pollution 2:21-30.

Delaune, R.D., C.J. Smith, W.H. Patrick, Jr., J.W. Fleeger, and M.D. Tolley. 1984. Effect of oil on salt marsh biota: methods for restoration. Environmental Pollution 36:207-227.

Fedorak, P.M. and D.W.S. Westlake. 1981. Microbial degradation of aromatics and saturates in Prudhoe Bay crude oil as determined by glass capillary gas chromatography. Canadian Journal of Microbiology 27:432-443.

Ferrell, R.E., E.D. Seneca, and R.A. Linthurst. 1984. The effects of crude oil on the growth of *Spartina alterniflora* Loisel and *Spartina cynosuroides* (L.) Roth. Journal of Experimental Marine Biology and Ecology 83:27-29.

Fricke, A.H., H.F. Henning, and M.J. Orren. Relationship between oil pollution and psammolittoral meiofauna density of two South African beaches. Marine Environmental Research 5:59-77.

Guenther, T., U. Dornberger, and W. Fritsche. 1996. Effects of ryegrass on biodegradation of hydrocarbons in soil. Chemosphere, 33(2): 203-215.

Hambrick, G.A., R.D. DeLaune, and W.H. Patrick, Jr. 1980. Effect of estuarine sediment pH and oxidation-reduction potential on microbial hydrocarbon degradation. Applied & Environmental Microbiology 40:365-369.

Hampson, G.R. and G.T. Moul. 1978. No. 2 fuel oil spill in Bourne, Massachusetts: immediate assessment of the effects on marine invertebrates and a 3 year study of growth and recovery of a salt marsh. Journal Fisheries Research Board of Canada 33:731-740.

Henry C.B. and E.B. Overton. 1993. Chemical composition and source-fingerprinting of depositional oil from the Kuwait oil fires. Proceedings of the 1993 Oil Spill Conference, API Washington, D.C., pp. 407-414.

Henry, C.B., P.O. Roberts, and E.B. Overton. 1993. Characterization of Chronic Sources and Impacts of Tar Along the Louisiana Coast. U.S. Dept. of the Interior, Minerals Management Service, Gulf of Mexico OCS Regional Office, New Orleans, La. OCS Study MMS 93-0046, 64 pp.

Hershner, C. and J. Lake. 1977. Effects of chronic oil pollution on a salt marsh grass community. Marine Biology 56:163-173.

Hershner, C. and K. Moore. 1977. Effects of the Chesapeake Bay oil spill on salt marshes of the lower bay. *Proceeding of the 1977 Oil Spill Conference*, American Petroleum Institute, Washington, D.C., pp. 529-33.

Holt, S., S. Rabalais, N. Rabalais, S. Cornelius, and J.S. Holland. 1978. Effects of an oil spill on salt marshes at Harbo Island, Texas. Proceedings of Concentrated Assessment of Ecological Impacts of Oil Spills, American Institute of Biological Science, Special Science Program, Keystone, Colorado, pp. 344-352

Hood, M.A. and S.P. Meyers. 1978. Chitin degradation in estuarine environments and implications in crustacean biology. In: Muzzarelli, A.A. and E.R. Pariser (eds.), Proceedings of the First International Conference on Chitin, Cambridge, MA, MIT Sea Grant Program, Massachusetts Institute of Technology, pp. 563-569.

Hurst, C.J., R.C. Sims, J.L. Sims, D.L. Sorensen, J.E. Mclean, and S. Huling. 1996. Polycyclic aromatic hydrocarbon biodegradation as a function of oxygen tension in contaminated soil. Journal of Hazardous Materials 51:193-208.

Jensen, H.Z. 1930. Actinomycetes in Danish Soils. *Soil Science* 30: 59-77.

Jorgensen, K.S., J. Puustinen, and A.M. Suortti. 2000. Bioremediation of petroleum hydrocarbon-contaminated soil by composting in biopiles. Environmental Pollution 107:245-254.

Kling, J. 1997. Phytoremediation of organics moving rapidly into field trials. *Environ. Sci. Tech.* 31:129.

Krebs, C.T. and C.E. Tanner. 1981. Restoration of oiled marshes through sediment stripping and Spartina propagation. Proceeding of the 1981 Oil Spill Conference, American Petroleum Institute, Washington, DC, pp. 375-385.

Lee, R.F., B. Dornseif, F. Gonsoulin, K. Tenore, and R. Hanson. 1981. Fate and effects of a heavy fuel oil spill on a Georgia salt marsh. Marine Environmental Research 5:125-143.

Lee, K, and E.M. Levy. 1987. Enhanced biodegradation of a light crude oil in sandy beaches. Proceedings of the 1987 Oil Spill Conference, American Petroleum Institute, Washington, D.C., pp. 411-416.

Lee, K and E.M. Levy. 1991. Bioremediation: waxy crude oils stranded on low-energy shorelines. Proceedings of 1991 Oil Spill Conference, American Petroleum Institute, Washington, D.C., pp. 524-541.

Lee, K, G.H. Tremblay, and E.M. Levy. 1993. Bioremediation: Application of slow release fertilizers on low-energy shorelines. Proceedings of the 1993 Oil Spill Conference, American Petroleum Institute, Washington, D.C., pp. 449-454.

Li, Y., J.T. Morris, and D.C. Yoch. 1990. Chronic low level hydrocarbon amendments stimulate plant growth and microbial activity in salt-marsh microcosms. Journal of Applied Ecology 27:159-171.

Lin Q. and I.A. Mendelssohn. 1996. A comparative investigation of the effects of Louisiana crude oil on the vegetation of fresh, brackish, and salt marsh. Marine Pollution Bulletin 32:202-209.

Lin, Q. and I.A. Mendelssohn. 1997. Phytoremediation for oil spill cleanup and habitat restoration in Louisiana coastal marshes: effects of marsh plant species and fertilizer. Louisiana Applied Oil Spill Research and Development Program, OSRADP Technical Report Series 169-30-4164, 45 pp.

Lin, Q. and I.A. Mendelssohn. 1998a. Phytoremediation for oil spill cleanup: biostimulant and species effects. Louisiana Applied Oil Spill Research and Development Program, *OSRADP Technical Report Series* 169-30-4172, 31 pp.

Lin, Q. and I.A. Mendelssohn. 1998b. The combined effects of phytoremediation and biostimulation in enhancing habitat restoration and oil degradation of petroleum contaminated wetlands. Ecological Engineering 10:263-274.

Lin, Q., I.A. Mendelssohn, C.B. Henry, M.W. Hester, and E.C. Webb. 1999a. Effects of Oil Cleanup Methods on Ecological Recovery and Oil Degradation of *Phragmite* Marshes. Proceeding of the 1999 Oil Spill Conference. American Petroleum Institute, Washington, D.C., pp.511-518.

Lin, Q., I.A. Mendelssohn, and R.J. Siebeling. 1999b. Effects of fresh marsh species and inundation environment on phytoremediation of oil. Louisiana Applied Oil Spill Research and Development Program, OSRADP Technical Report Series 169-30-4177, 32 pp.

Lin, Q., I.A. Mendelssohn, C.B. Henry, P.O. Roberts, M.M. Walsh, E.B. Overton, and R.J. Portier. 1999c. Effects of bioremediation agents on oil degradation in mineral and sandy salt marsh sediments. *Environmental Technology* 20:825-837.

Lindstrom, J.E., R.C. Prince, J.C. Clark, M.J. Grossman, T.R. Yeager, J.F. Braddock, and E.J. Brown. 1991. Microbial populations and hydrocarbon biodegradation potentials in fertilized shoreline sediments affected by the Exxon Valdez oil spill. Applied and Environmental Microbiology 57:2514-22.

Lipczynskakochany, E. 1992. Degradation of nitrobenzene and nitrophenols by means of advanced oxidation processes in a homogeneous phase - photolysis in the presence of hydrogen-peroxide versus the Fenton Reaction. Chemosphere 24:1369-1380.

Liste Hans, H. and M. Alexander. 2000a. Accumulation of phenanthrene and pyrene in rhizosphere soil. Chemosphere. 40(1):11-14.

Liste, Hans, H. and M. Alexander. 2000b. Plant promoted pyrene degradation in soil. Chemosphere. 40(1):7-10.

Lovley, D.R., J.C. Woodward, and F.H. Chapelle. 1994. Stimulated anoxic biodegradation of aromatic hydrocarbons using Fe(III) ligands. Nature 370:128-131.

Lytle, J.S. and T.F. Lytle. 1987. The role of *Juncus roemerianus* in cleanup of oil-polluted sediments. *Proceeding of the 1987 Oil Spill Conference*, American Petroleum Institute, Washington, DC, pp. 495-501.

Maki, H., T. Sasaki, E. Sasaki, M. Ishihara, M. Goto, and S. Harayama. 1999. Use of wastewater sludge for the amendment of crude oil bioremediation in meso-scale beach simulating tanks. Environmental Technology 20:625-632.

McKee, K.L. and I.A. Mendelssohn. 1995. A review of the methods and ecological consequences of substrate aeration for the enhancement of oil bioremediation in wetlands. Report to the Marine Spill Response Corporation, Washington. DC. 31 pp.

McKee, K.L., I.A. Mendelssohn, and M.W. Hester. 1988. Reexamination of pore water sulfide concentration and redox potentials near the aerial roots of *Rhizophora mangle* and *Avicennia germinans*. American Journal of Botany 75:1352-1358.

McMillen, S.J. 1991. Qualitative on-site monitoring of bioremediation - summary of survey results. Unpublished presentation at 1991 Bioremediation Workshop, Las Vegas, NV.

Martin, J.P. 1950. Use of acid, rose bengal and streptomycin in the plate method for estimating soil fungi. Soil Science 69:215-233.

Mearns, A. 1991. Observations of an oil spill bioremediation activity in Galveston Bay, Texas. NOAA Technical Memorandum NOS OMA 57, Seattle Washington, 38 p.

Mendelssohn, I.A., M.W. Hester, and C. Sasser. 1990. The effect of a Louisiana crude oil discharge from a pipeline break on the vegetation of a southeast Louisiana brackish marsh. Oil and Chemical Pollution 7:1-15.

Mendelssohn, I.A., M.W. Hester, and J.M. Hill. 1993. Assessing the recovery of coastal wetlands from oil spills. Proceeding of the 1993 Oil Spill Conference. American Petroleum Institute, Washington, D.C., 141-145.

Mikesell, M.D., R.H. Olsen, and J.J. Kukor. 1991. Stratification of anoxic BTEX-degrading bacteria at three petroleum-contaminated sites. In Situ Bioreclamation Symposium, San Diego, CA, pp. 351-362.

Nance, J.M. 1991. Effects of oil/gas field produced water on the macrobenthic community in a small gradient estuary. Hydrobiologia 220:189-204.

Nohrstedt, H.O., K. Arnebrant, E. Baath, and B. Soderstrom. 1989. Changes in carbon content, respiration rate, ATP content and microbial biomass in nitrogen fertilized pine forest soils in Sweden. Canadian Journal of Forest Research 19:323-328.

Parsons, T.R., Y. Maita, and C.M. Lalli. 1984. A Manual of Chemical and Biological Methods for Seawater analysis: Method 1.6. Pergamon Press. 173p.

Patrick W.H., R.P. Gambrell, and S.P. Faulkner. 1996. Redox measurements of soil. Methods of Soil Analysis, Part 3, Chemical Method-SSSA Book Series No. 5. Soil Science Society of America and American Society of Agro., pp. 1225-1273.

Pearson, T.H. and R. Rosenberg. 1978. Macrobenthic succession in relation to organic enrichment and pollution of the marine environment. Oceanography and Marine Biology Annual Review 16:229-311.

Prince, R.C., R.E. Bare, G.N. George, C.E. Haith, M.J. Grossman, J.R. Lute, D.L. Elmendorf, B.V.Minak, J.D. Seniue, L.G. Keim, R.R. Chianelli, S.M. Hinton, and A.R. Teal. 1993. The effect of bioremediation on the microbial populations of oiled beaches in Prince William Sound, Alaska. Proceeding of the 1993 Oil Spill Conference, American Petroleum Institute, Washington, DC, pp. 469-475.

Rabalais, N.N., B.A. McKee, D.J. Reed, and J.C. Means. 1992. Fate and effects of produced water discharges in coastal Louisiana, Gulf of Mexico, USA. In: Ray, J.P. and R.R. Engelhart (eds.), Produced Water, Plenum Press, New York, pp. 355-369.

Reilley, K.A., K.M. Banks, and A.P. Schwab. 1996. Dissipation of polycyclic aromatic hydrocarbons in the rhizosphere. *J. Environ. Qual.*, 25:212-219.

Reynolds, C.M., D.C. Wolf, T.J. Gentry, L.B. Perry, C.S. Pidgeon, B.A. Koenen, H.B. Rogers, and C.A. Beyrouty. 1999. Plant enhancement of indigenous soil micro-organisms: A low-cost treatment of contaminated soils. Polar Record, 35:33-40.

Roberge, M.R. 1976. Respiration rates for determining the effects of urea on the soil surface organic horizon of a black spruce stand. Canadian Journal of Microbiology 22:1328-1335.

Roques, D.E., E.B. Overton, and C.B. Henry. 1994. Using gas chromatography/mass spectroscopy fingerprint analyses to document process and progress of oil degradation. Journal of Environmental Quality 23:851-855.

Safferman, S.I. 1991. Selection of nutrients to enhance biodegradation for the remediation of oil spilled on beaches. Proceedings of the 1991 Oil Spill Conference, American Petroleum Institute, Washington, D.C., pp. 571-576.

Salmon, C., J.L. Crabos, J.P. Sambuco, J.M. Bessiere, A. Basseres, P. Caumette, and J.C. Baccou. 1998. Artificial wetland performances in the purification efficiency of hydrocarbon wastewater. Water, Air and Soil Pollution. 104:313-329.

Salt, D.E., M. Blaylock, N.P. Kumar, V. Dushenkuv, B.D. Ensley, I. Chet, and I. Raskin. 1995. Phytoremediation: A novel strategy for the removal of toxic metals from the environment using plants. Biotechnology, 13:468-474.

Sanders, H.L., J.F. Grassle, G.R. Hampton, L.S. Morse, P.S. Garner, and C.C. Jones. 1980. Anatomy of an oil spill: long term effects from the grounding of barge *Florida* off West Falmouth, Massachusetts. Journal of Marine Research 38:265-380.

SAS. 1990. SAS/STAT User's Guide Volume 2, SAS Institute Inc., Cary, NC. pp. 891-996.

Sauer T. and P. Boehm. 1991. The use of defensible analytical chemical measurements for oil spill natural resource damage assessment. Proceedings of the 1991 Oil Spill Conference, American Petroleum Institute, Washington, D.C., pp. 363-369.

Scherbarth, L.L. 1984. Analysis of Chitin Colonization with Scanning Electron Microscopy, Microbial Biomass, and ATP/FDA Approaches. Louisiana State University, Baton Rouge, Louisiana.

Scherrer, P. and G. Mille. 1990. Biodegradation of crude oil in experimentally-polluted clayey and sandy mangrove soils. Oil and Chemical Pollution 6:163-176.

Schnoor, J.L., L.A. Licht, S.C. McCutcheon, N.L. Wolfe, and L.H. Carreira. 1995. Phytoremediation of organic and nutrient contaminants. *Environ. Sci, Technol.*, 29(7):318-323.

Schwab. A.P., A.A. Al-Assi, and M.K. Banks. 1998. Adsorption of naphthalene onto plant roots. Journal of Environmental Quality. 27 (1):220-224.

Smirnoff, N. and R.M.M. Crawford. 1983. Variation in the structure and response to flooding of root aerenchyma in some wetland plants. *Annals of Botany*, 51:237-249.

Spies, R.B. 1987. The biological effects of petroleum hydrocarbons in the sea: assessments from the field and microcosms. In: Boesch, D.F. and N.N. Rabalais (eds.), Long Term Environmental Effects of Offshore Oil and Gas Development, Elservier, London, pp. 411-467.

Stomp, A.M., K.H. Han, and M.P. Gordon. 1983. Genetic improvement of tree species for remediation of hazardous wastes. *In Vitro Cellular & Developmental Biology-Plant.* 29:227-232.

Swannell, R.P.J., D. Mitshell, G. Lethbridge, D. Jones, D. Heath, M. Hagley, M. Jones, S. Petch, R. Milne, R. Croxford, and K. Lee. 1999. A field demonstration of the efficacy of bioremediation to treat oiled shorelines following the Sea Empress incident. Environmental Technology, 20:863-873.

Tabak, H.H., J.R. Haines, A.D. Venosa, and J.A. Glaser. 1991. Enhancement of biodegradation of Alaskan weathered crude oil components by indigenous micrbiota with the use of fertilizers and nutrients. Proceedings of the 1991 Oil Spill Conference, American Petroleum Institute, Washington, D.C., pp. 583-590.

Teal, J.M., and J.W. Kanwisher. 1966. Gas transport in the marsh grass *Spartina alterniflora. J. of Exp. Bot.,* 17:355-61.

Thirukkumaran, C.M. and D. Perkingson. 2000. Microbial respiration, biomass, metabolic quotient and litter decomposition in a lodgepole pine forest floor amended with nitrogen and phosphorous fertilizers. Soil Biology and Biochemistry 32:59-66.

U.S. Congress, Office of Technology Assessment. 1991. Bioremediation for marine oil spills. Background Paper OTA-BP-O-70, Washington, D.C. U.S. Government Printing Office. 32 pp.

United States Environmental Protection Agency. 1984. Permit Guidance Manual on Hazardous Waste Land Treatment Demonstrations (Draft). Office of Solid Waste and Emergency Response.

Venosa, A.D., J.R. Haines, and D.M. Allen. 1992. Efficacy of commercial inocula in enhancing biodegradation of weathered crude oil contaminating a Prince William Sound beach. Journal of Industrial Microbiology 10:1-11.

Venosa, A.D., M.T. Suidan, B.A. Wrenn, K.L. Strohmeier, J.R. Haines, B.L. Eberhart, D. King, and E. Holder. 1996. Bioremediation of an experimental oil spill on the shoreline of Delaware Bay. Environmental Science and Technology 30:1764-1775.

von Caemmerer, S. and G.D. Farquhar. 1981. Some relationship between the biochemistry of photosynthesis and the gas exchange of leaves. Planta 153:376-387.

Walworth, J.L. and C.M. Reynolds. 1995. Bioremediation of a petroleum-contaminated cryic soil: Effects of phosphorus, nitrogen, and temperature. Journal of Soil Contamination, 4:299-310.

Wang, Y.T. and J.L. Latchaw. 1990. Anaerobic biodegradability and toxicity of hydrogen-peroxide oxidation-products of phenols. Research Journal of Water Pollution Control 62:234-238.

Williams, C.M., J.L. Grimes, and R.L. Mikkelsen. 1999. The use of poultry litter as co-substrate and source of inorganic nutrients and microorganisms for the ex situ biodegradation of petroleum compounds. Poultry Science 78:956-964.

Wilsey, B.J., K.L. McKee, and I.A. Mendelssohn. 1992. Effects of increased elevation and macro- and micronutrient additions on *Spartina alterniflora* transplant success in salt-marsh dieback area in Louisiana. Environmental Management 16:505-511.

Wilson, D.L.P., P.C. Adamo, and E.J. Bouwer. 1999. Aromatic hydrocarbon biodegradation with mixtures of $O_2$ and $NO^{3-}$ as electron acceptors. Environmental Engineering Science 16:487-500.

Wollum, A.G. 1982. Cultural methods for soil microorganisms. In: Page, A.L. (ed.), Methods of Soil Analysis, Part 2: Chemical and Microbiological Properties, 2nd ed., Madison, Wisconsin, Soil Science Society of America, Inc., pp. 781-802.

Wornald, A.P. 1976. Effects of a spill of marine diesel on the meiofauna of a sandy beach at Picnic Bay, Hong Kong. Environmental Pollution 11:117-130.

Wright, A.L., R.W. Weaver, and J.W. Webb. 1997. Oil bioremediation in salt marsh mesocosms as influenced by N and P fertilization, flooding, and season. *Water, Air and Soil Pollution* 95:179-191.

**EFFECTS OF BIOREMEDIATION ON MICROBIAL BIOMASS**

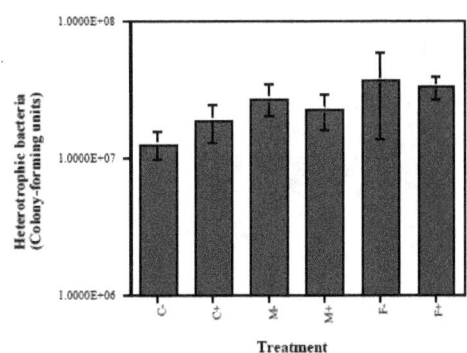

Figure A1. Effect of bioremediation agents and oil application on heterotrophic bacteria three days after the treatment. Values are reported in colony-forming units per gram (dry weight) of soil with standard error. C: control; M: microbial seeding; F: fertilizer. Plus signs indicate oiling and minus signs no oiling.

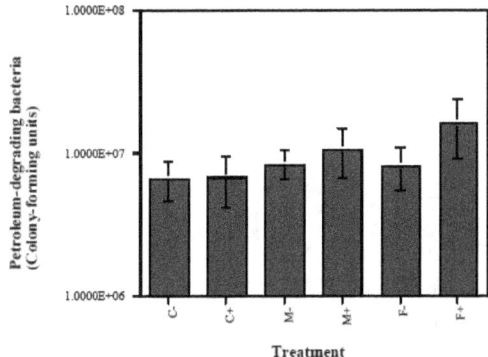

Figure A2. Effect of bioremediation agents and oil on petroleum-degrading bacteria three days after treatment. Values are reported in colony-forming units per gram (dry weight) of soil with standard error. C: control; M: microbial addition; F: fertilizer. Plus signs indicate oiling and minus signs no oiling.

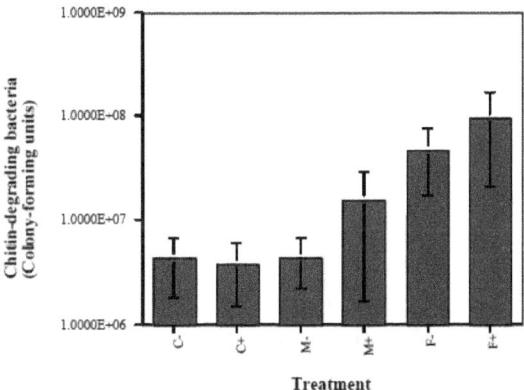

Figure A3. Effect of bioremediation agents and oil on chitin-degrading bacteria 3 days after treatment. Values are reported in colony-forming units per gram (dry weight) of soil with standard error. C: control; M: microbial addition; F: fertilizer. Plus signs indicate oiling and minus signs no oiling.

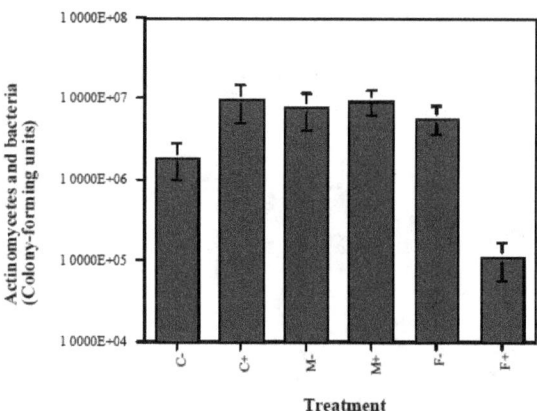

Figure A4. Effect of bioremediation agents and oil on cellulose-degrading actinomycetes and bacteria 3 days after treatment. Values are reported in colony-forming units per gram (dry weight) of soil with standard error. C: control; M: microbial addition; F: fertilizer. Plus signs indicate oiling and minus signs no oiling.

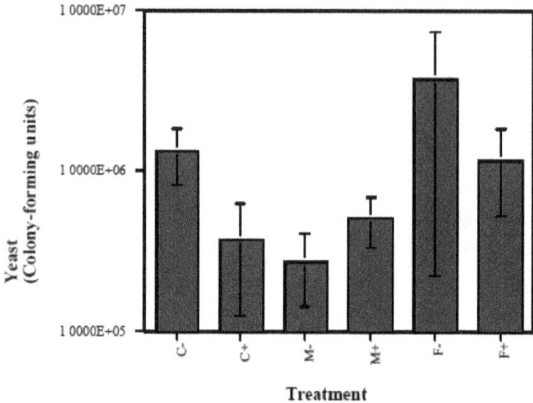

Figure A5. Effect of bioremediation agents and oil on yeast populations 3 days after treatment. Values are reported in colony-forming units per gram (dry weight) of soil with standard error. C: control; M: microbial addition; F: fertilizer. Plus signs indicate oiling and minus signs no oiling.

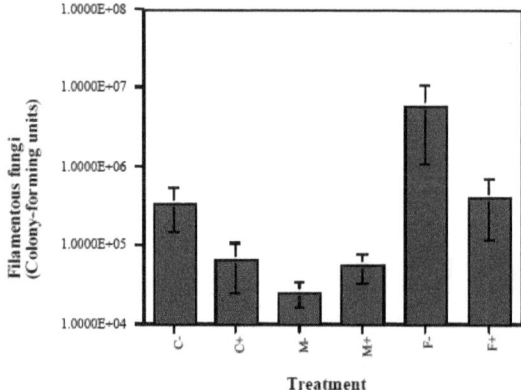

Figure A6. Effect of bioremediation agents and oil on filamentous fungi 3 days after treatment. Values are reported in colony-forming units per gram (dry weight) of soil with standard error. C: control; M: microbial addition; F: fertilizer. Plus signs indicate oiling and minus signs no oiling.

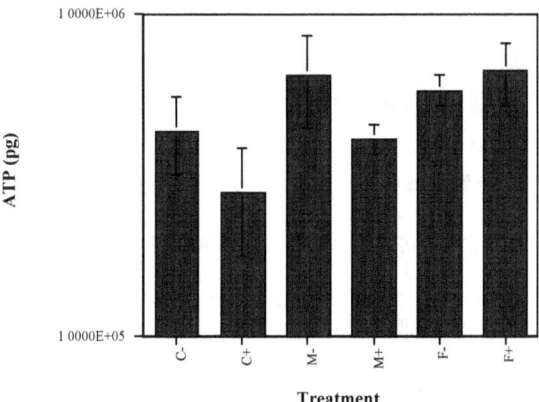

Figure A7. Effect of bioremediation agents and oil on microbial biomass three days after treatment. Values are reported in picograms of ATP per gram (dry weight) of soil with standard error. C: control; M: microbial addition; F: fertilizer. Plus signs indicate oiling and minus signs no oiling.

# APPENDIX B

## OIL MORPHOLOGY DEFINITIONS

Surface oil in the marsh sods expressed changes in surface oil character, which could not be attributed to biodegradation:

(1) **Oil Mousse:** The term refers to the brown to light brown coat or cover which wipes off easily and has a creamy consistency. This Oil Mousse is sometimes a little tacky. In the flooded series this creamy texture was most likely enhanced by the mixing of oil and water, hence "Oil Mousse."

A similar oil morphology was observed during the Quality Control Monitoring Program, was referred to as Oil Cream, and was shown not to indicate biodegradation but rather a chemical reaction with the bioremediation product.

Oil Mousse was a common change in surface oil characteristics during the first observations in the flooded and drained M-treated series and in the flooded C-, F-, and OF-treated series. However, Oil Mousse was found up to seven weeks after product-application. Because of its unweathered character, the presence of this oil morphology several weeks after oil-application was attributed to renewed exposure of fresher oil after a layer of the surface oil had been degraded.

(2) **White Surface Coating:** This coating appears as a white film covering oil and surface sediments. The presence of this surface coating was unique to the OF-treated marsh sods and was attributed to the application of the oxidant.

White surface coating was observed on the surface of all marsh sods after OF-application. This coat was present in both flooded and drained marsh sods but was better mixed into the sediments in the flooded series. In the drained series, this coating was observed up to five weeks after product-application. In the flooded series, the last observation of this coating was observed on the eighth day after product-application.

A change in surface oil character indicative of biodegradation was observed in all treatments and replicates (subsurface oil did not occur in any of the marsh sods). Surface oil character changes were often first detected through a change in color of the oil, usually from black to brown or darker to lighter shades of brown. In addition to this initial indication of oil change, color changes in surface oiling were commonly associated with a change in the consistency of the oil. The latter was the most important oil morphology indicator of degradation.

Unfortunately, samples of altered oil were not taken for microbiological and/or detailed oil analyses to confirm enhanced microbial activity and enhanced biodegradation. However, the oil morphologies observed in the current study and defined below were largely consistent with some of the oil changes observed during the Exxon Valdez Quality Control Monitoring Program for which such samples were taken. For example, samples of oil defined as Organic Coat and Paste during this monitoring program were the most highly biodegraded oil samples collected throughout the area of oil impact at the time and confirmed that the visual and tactile changes in surface oil observed during the surveys were indicative of biodegradation (Debusschere *et al.* 1991; McMillen 1991).

Other oil morphologies indicative of advanced biodegradation resulting from bioremediation-applications observed during this monitoring program were not observed in the current study. However, oil morphologies were noted to be partly dictated by the substrate and pre-application oil character (Debusschere *et al.* 1991). As the current study focused on salt marsh habitats and marsh sods that are relatively uniform in substrate, the limited number of oil changes indicative of enhanced biodegradation in the current study are most likely the result of the similarities in marsh sod substrate.

The following provides a list of definitions of oil morphologies observed during the current study. Reference to previously identified oil morphologies and associated oil chemistry and microbial analyses (Debusschere *et al*. 1991, McMillen 1991) are made when applicable.

(1) **Organic Coat:** The oil is dark to light-brown and rubs off very easily in a semi-liquid consistency without leaving any oily residue. In some cases only a surface layer of the oil had changed to an Organic Coat. Only this surface layer then constitutes the Organic Coat, which, when wiped off, leaves a tacky and tarry residue on the sediment surface.

Several samples of Organic Coat were analyzed during the Quality Control Monitoring Program. The oil analysis of these samples substantiated that all were extremely biodegraded. Dense populations of algae, fungi, and/or bacteria were present in samples of Organic Coat.

Organic Coat was a common oil change throughout the duration of this study and occurred in drained and flooded series for all four treatments. The first occurrence of Organic Coat in the drained flooding regime was observed on day 8 in the OF-treated marsh sods. In the flooded series, Organic Coat was first observed three weeks after product-application in the OF-, M-, and C-series.

(2) **Paste**: As is the case for Organic Coat, the oil comes off when rubbed but leaves a tacky residue of a more solid consistency. This layer of degrading oil sometimes occurs as thin flakes and can be rolled into a tubular clayey mass.

Paste was found to be substantially biodegraded during the Quality Control Monitoring Program. Dense populations of algae, fungi, and/or bacteria were found in Paste samples.

Paste was most commonly associated with the drained series. The first occurrence of Paste in the drained flooding regime was observed on day 6 in the OF-treated marsh sods. In the flooded series, Paste was not observed until seven weeks after product-application. At that time, only the F- and C-series were characterized by this oil change. Paste never was observed in the flooded OF-application.

(3) **Organic Film**: The oil is brown and rubs off very easily without leaving any residue. The consistency of this film is more viscous when compared with the semi-liquid consistency of Organic Coat.

During the Quality Control Monitoring Program, this oil character was usually found in the subsurface. No samples of Organic Film were available for analysis.

Organic Film was observed in all flooded product-applications. First occurrence of the oil character was noted three weeks into the experiment in the flooded OF- and F-treated marsh sods. In the M- and C- treated sods, Organic Film was first observed seven weeks after product-application. In the drained flooding regime, Organic Film was only observed in the OF-series (first at week 5) and the M-series (only at week 12).

(4) **Powder**: The term refers to a layer of surface sediments in the marsh sods with a powdery consistency. The sediments rub off very easily without leaving any residue and do not create a sheen when submerged in water. This oil change was termed Powder because of similarities with Powder found during the Quality Control Monitoring Program where it was described as a brown dry coat, which also rubbed off very easily without leaving any residue. This dry coat had a consistency very much like a "chocolate cake-mix" (Debusschere *et al*. 1991).

During the Quality Control Monitoring Program, Powder was observed on boulders and bedrock from which it could be easily blown away or washed away with water. These observations indicated that Powder was substantially biodegraded. Unfortunately, because of the transient nature of this oil morphology, no samples of Powder were available for analysis.

Powder only was observed in the drained OF-treated marsh sods at week 12. Although Paste, Organic Coat, and Organic Film sometimes had a powdery feel in the OF-treated series during earlier observations, this consistency was attributed to the presence of the oxidant rather than advanced biodegradation.

(5) **Brown Flakes**: The term is used in association with water. Dark-Brown Flakes are composed of biomass and oil floating on the water surface. Brown Flakes are usually characterized by a jagged edge.

An identical oil character was observed during the Quality Control Monitoring Program and was identified as an indicator of enhanced biodegradation for subsurface oil.

The only occurrence of this oil character during the current study was in association with an oil sheen in the flooded OF-treated marsh sods at day 2 of the experiment.

During the Quality Control Monitoring Program, Paste, Organic Coat, and Organic Film sometimes had a silty feel. The siltiness of these surface oil characters was noted to be most likely the result of the presence of fine sediments mixed in the oil, which can be observed by touch after the oil has reached a certain degree of biodegradation. . This observation was not repeated during the current study. However, the lack of coarser sediments in marsh sediments may have prevented this characteristic to occur.

## The Department of the Interior Mission

As the Nation's principal conservation agency, the Department of the Interior has responsibility for most of our nationally owned public lands and natural resources.  This includes fostering sound use of our land and water resources; protecting our fish, wildlife, and biological diversity; preserving the environmental and cultural values of our national parks and historical places; and providing for the enjoyment of life through outdoor recreation. The Department assesses our energy and mineral resources and works to ensure that their development is in the best interests of all our people by encouraging stewardship and citizen participation in their care. The Department also has a major responsibility for American Indian reservation communities and for people who live in island territories under U.S. administration.

## The Minerals Management Service Mission

As a bureau of the Department of the Interior, the Minerals Management Service's (MMS) primary responsibilities are to manage the mineral resources located on the Nation's Outer Continental Shelf (OCS), collect revenue from the Federal OCS and onshore Federal and Indian lands, and distribute those revenues.

Moreover, in working to meet its responsibilities, the **Offshore Minerals Management Program** administers the OCS competitive leasing program and oversees the safe and environmentally sound exploration and production of our Nation's offshore natural gas, oil and other mineral resources.  The MMS **Minerals Revenue Management** meets its responsibilities by ensuring the efficient, timely and accurate collection and disbursement of revenue from mineral leasing and production due to Indian tribes and allottees, States and the U.S. Treasury.

The MMS strives to fulfill its responsibilities through the general guiding principles of:  (1) being responsive to the public's concerns and interests by maintaining a dialogue with all potentially affected parties and (2) carrying out its programs with an emphasis on working to enhance the quality of life for all Americans by lending MMS assistance and expertise to economic development and environmental protection.